Praise for "The Abandoned"

Like so many survivors of the Holocaust, Evelyn Romanowsky Ripp's first memories are of a world that is lost forever, destroyed amid savage brutality. Her home town, Lachva, is only a small speck on most maps, yet it was the center of a vibrant Jewish life before the war. Its pre-war life is described here with great charm, evoking a lost age, a lost world. In 1942 that world came to an abrupt and vicious end. With great feeling, Evelyn Ripp tells the story of the Lachva ghetto. Her poems tell much more, starting with the line: "I've been silent so long." She is silent no more. All those interested in Jewish history will be grateful to her for her words and verses.

Sir Martin Gilbert
Biographer & noted Historian

Poetry is not the conventional genre for describing the Holocaust, but here it is used with great skill and passion. The reader will long remember these beautiful poems. *The Abandoned: A Life Apart from Life* is an important contribution to Holocaust literature and I highly recommend it.

Dr. Stephen M. Berk
Professor of History & Chair of Holocaust and Jewish Studies
Union College

Evelyn Ripp's poetry takes us to the edge of the abyss and forces us to look down. The immediacy and intimacy of Evelyn's poems humanize the statistics, helping us to understand her experiences and to empathize with her attempts to integrate them into her still-haunted life today. This volume makes an excellent addition to any high school or university course on the Holocaust and will enrich the background of any adult interested in this subject.

Karen Shawn, Ph.D., Educational Consultant
American Friends of the Ghetto Fighters' Museum

Evelyn Romanowsky Ripp allows us a glimpse of the inner life of a survivor. Her poetic wonderings about God's absence/presence and remembrances and evocations of people and places are the underpinnings of this book and of her life – to learn to "at once, remember and forget."

Dr. Gloria F. Waldman-Schwartz, Professor
York College and The Cuny Graduate Center

To Phyllis Markowitz —
For your caring.
All best wishes.
Evelyn Ripp
November 3, 2017

The
Abandoned

A Life Apart from Life

Evelyn Romanowsky Ripp

COMTEQ
PUBLISHING
MARGATE, NEW JERSEY

Published by:
    ComteQ Publishing
    A division of ComteQ Communications, LLC
    P.O. Box 3046
    Margate, New Jersey 08402
    609-487-9000 • Fax 609-822-4098
    Email: publisher@ComteQcom.com
    Website: www.ComteQpublishing.com

ISBN 0-9674074-7-8
Library of Congress Control Number: 2003115396

Book and cover design by Rob Huberman

Printed in the United States of America
10 9 8 7 6 5 4 3 2 1

For my husband, Norbert,
whose encouragement and support
have helped me find my voice,
and for our children and grandchildren.

Dedicated to all people who uphold
the truth about the Holocaust.

"The only thing necessary for the triumph of evil is for good men to do nothing"

Edmund Burke

"Silence gives consent."

Oliver Goldsmith

Contents

Poems (continued)

Foreword

It is clear from the outset that Evelyn Ripp writes to bear witness – to record the sordid truth in all its tragic, yet often bittersweet detail. Truth and honesty are hard won. Both require extraordinary courage to face unbearable pain in the service of history and humanity.

As human beings our wish is to hide, to protect our selves from what we know, to protect our families from what we saw and felt. We work to block, to forget, to hide, and when forgetting is impossible, we silence ourselves. We lock the pain deep in our psyches and hearts and bear it alone – hopeful that silence will quiet it – or, at least contain it. But, the Shoah pain in its breadth and scourge cannot be contained.

Evelyn Ripp's *The Abandoned* recounts in searing detail the horrors of Nazi brutality toward an innocent people. We wish to turn away from such vast a horror. But Ripp forces the reader to feel the cruelty, and to be repelled and terrified each step along the way.

With excruciating honesty, the writer reveals that life so that we ache, feel assaulted, and are filled with rage, yet rendered powerless. Ripp's gift lies in her choice of detail, her willingness to tell stories that touch us most profoundly: fathers sleeping with axes under their pillows, the killing of a young man for his eyeglasses, the heartbreak of a mother's and sister's disappearance, the call for people to present themselves before firing squads, the steady and systematic destruction of a town. All of this called forth from the life of an eleven-year-old girl. We are forced to live beside the children for two years in the forest, foraging for food with them, and then she startles us with childish play in the midst of deprivation.

As readers, we are threatened then empowered by a spirit that is vulnerable, and by the writer's enduring love of beauty, humor,

compassion and the life force that celebrates small victories and occasional kindness. We are grateful to the Christians who hid Jews, and we revel in the ghetto's resistance and uprising: its will to destroy itself rather than face extermination. Together with her, we are terrorized by nightmares, long to buy a Red Dress, rail at God *Where were You when gold teeth/Were ripped from jaws/When women and children were shot/And buried half alive,* feel the survivor's guilt *My joy is joy confined,* and again *We ran for our lives/Under German fire/They fell/And I go on/I wake tormented/I live in place of them.*
     And later,

> *But for the record,*
> *There will always be*
> *In the convex mirror*
> *Of the Shoah,*
> *The likeness of me,*
> *Eyes bursting toward Heaven,*
> *Mouth pried open*
> *By a scream.*

Joan Cusack Handler
Psychologist and Poet

A Word of Explanation

The Holocaust was a collective experience, but it was also an individual experience. Each survivor has his own unique story to tell.

This memoir begins with a brief description of my happy childhood in the eastern Polish *shtetl* of Lachva. It came to an abrupt end on September 17, 1939, when Soviet troops occupied the town. The oppressive new regime halted all organized Jewish activities and set up a police state, deporting "undesirables" to Siberia. Two years later, Nazi troops took over Lachva. Since the Russian retreat several days earlier, peasants had attacked Jews at random. We Jews hoped that the "civilized" Germans would restore order. Instead, on April 1, 1942, the Jews of Lachva were confined to a ghetto. Food was scarce and disease was rampant. Our men and women were forced to work as slave laborers. Finally the ghetto was "liquidated" by German mobile squads.

After the defeat of Germany, the Nazi murderers who killed the Jews of Lachva and surrounding communities were brought to trial for their crimes. Included is a summary of the legal proceedings against them, which were translated from the German. Justice was not served; the murderers got no more than a slap on the wrist.

Finally there is a description of my return to Lachva in 2001, and my visit to the mass grave where my mother, my sister and twenty-five family members lie buried together with the other two-thousand people who perished.

The poems, arranged chronologically, focus in on and expand specific events. Though each poem is self-contained, they are interdependent. Together the prose and the poems convey my story as best as I can tell it.

I mean to preserve my Shoah experiences and to pass on to the reader some insight into that overwhelming event.

E.R.

11

A Life
Apart from Life

A Life Apart from Life

Sometimes I feel as though I lived my real life then – a life apart from the years which have passed since its destruction in 1942. Memories never cease rising from deep within me, begging to be preserved, to be passed on.

There once was a small town in eastern Poland called Lachva, (Polish, Lachwa) the *shtetl* of my birth, situated near Pinsk, (now Belarus), in the Polesie wood and swampy lowland region, near the Pripet River. Lachva was Polish from 1569 to 1793 and 1920 to 1939. It was Russian from 1793 to 1920, and again since 1939. By this time it had some 6,000 inhabitants. Its Jewish community dated back well over 300 years, and by 1939 made up approximately one third of the population.

The houses in our town consisted mostly of one room with a dirt floor and walls plastered and whitewashed, under a thatch roof. The toilet facility was an outhouse in the back yard. Houses were heated with wood-burning wall ovens. Drinking water was drawn from a well, but water for all other purposes had to be brought from the river. Yosele-the-water-carrier was an essential member of our community.

A coachman would take people from one *shtetl* to another in a wagon in the summer, and a sled in the winter. The streets were unpaved and a heavy rain would transform them into a sea of mud, or *blotes*. The mud stood inches high and there were wheel tracks and imprints of horses' hoofs where carriages passed. Wooden carts with big spoked wheels would often sink right up to their hubs and get stuck in the mud. In the summertime, horses' hoofs or cattle returning from pasture would kick up dense clouds of dust over the roads of dried mud.

During the stillness of summer, with no school to attend, children stayed close to home. My mother, my sisters and I would don our bathing suits – mine was maize with a multicolored butterfly in front, mother's was a navy blue wool tank style – and go swimming. The less affluent women would swim in their linen slips. These garments, upon contacting the water, billowed around the bather like an inflated bubble. Swimming was segregated. The women's section was in the shallower area of the lake. It was shaded by dense overhanging foliage and was always dark and cool. Only the loud shrieks and laughter of the bathers would pierce this peaceful setting.

I would be busy with my friends among whom I was a leader. Our favorite pastime was playing theater. After recruiting a group of grandmothers and great-grandmothers for an audience in the back yard, I would stand on a chair to introduce the performers one by one. We sang Yiddish, Hebrew, Polish and Russian songs, recited poems and danced. The elderly ladies were thoroughly entertained.

The center of our town was the *mark*, the market place. It was a cobbled square from which all streets emanated, like the spokes from the hub of a wheel. Some had wooden sidewalks. The *mark* was surrounded by stores. There was an apothecary, a fabric store, and general stores. My grandfather, Yankl Rabinovitch, with his two sons, Gershon and Shmuel Ber, were proprietors of the largest general store. They had plump burlap sacks of barley, rice, rye and wheat lined up in front. There were barrels of herring inside, various household needs, and even some few ready made items, such as berets and bathing suits, brought in from the large cities.

Once a week farmers and their families from the surrounding areas would bring their produce to market: fruits, vegetables, eggs and even live chickens. They bought their necessities from the Jewish shopkeepers. On that day the town was jammed with people and rearing and plunging horses. Everyone in our family was mobilized to help in our fabric store.

Lachva had no physician. There was a *feldsher*, a sort of paramedic who was able to write some prescriptions, which were filled at the apothecary. People trusted his practical experience. We also relied on well tried folk remedies. One of these was the application of *bankes* – cupping. This was performed exclusively by Esther-the-widow. Upon arrival at the bedside she would set up little glass suction cups, dab each with alcohol, heat it briefly over a flame and apply to the patient's back. When the cups were removed shortly after, there remained a red welt where each glass had been. Cupping was a popular healing tradition used to draw out fever or infection and to promote circulation.

My immediate family consisted of my parents, Moshe Zev and Menia Romanowsky, two sisters, Esther and Genia, and me, Cheva. Grandparents, great-grandparents and a host of relatives lived in town. The community was deeply inbred, and almost all were interrelated.

Though extremely close, we were not a demonstrative family. There seldom was any display of affection. Although my parents were strict disciplinarians, they provided us with a lot of love. They worried about us, were deeply concerned with our welfare, and were always there for us. They never quarreled in the presence of their children. By the example of their daily life they instilled in us their values: to be honest, respectful of our elders, to be modest and practice moderation.

Most people in Lachva were very poor and barely eked out a living. Time and again my sisters and I were reminded of the fact that not everyone had as much as we did. We lived in a comfortable five-room home, and ours was one of the very few houses in town that had electricity. We had the best of the available foods, as well as delicacies which my father brought from his buying trips to Lodz and Warsaw. When we were tempted to eat such things as grapes, bananas or salami in the presence of friends, most of whom had never seen these foods, mother would remind us that unless we were prepared to share, such luxuries should be eaten in private. Unlike most other youngsters, we had new outfits made for Passover and for the High Holidays. Twice a year mother would take us to the dressmaker and the shoemaker where we would select patterns and be measured for size.

Although father made frequent buying trips, he was at home most of the time. There was never a doubt that he was the boss in our house. We children were a little afraid of him because he also administered the more serious punishment... But there were always the gifts he brought us from his trips, the conversations at mealtime, the help with our school work, and last but not least, the trips to the outhouse.

No matter how sad we might have been at times, mother, ever cheerful, was always able to distract us. She met every challenge with optimism and humor. "Let's sing," she'd say, and lead off with her beautiful singing voice. When illness confined us to bed, she might give us a favorite alarm clock which would ring for us over and over, and teach us to tell time. Or, when we were a little older, she'd give us her outdated copy of the Old Church Slavonic Encyclopedia and permit us to cut out articles and pictures from it. In this way she got us interested in learning Russian. Being sick could be most enjoyable if it did not include the use of *bankes*...

One beautiful, crisp winter day, when my sisters and I were recovering from whooping cough, mother hired a coachman to take us on a journey to the neighboring town of Kozhangorodok for a "cure." The idea – to leave the whooping cough at our destination. The coachman arrived, and we, wearing layers of clothing and lined boots, were wrapped in blankets up to our chins as we took our places. He cracked his whip and the sled set off with the jingling of the horses' bells. And, by the time we got home, we really did feel all better.

Unlike mother, who had received a secular education and was graduated from the Russian *gymnasium* (high school), father received a parochial education at a prominent *yeshiva* in western Poland. Subsequently, because career choices for Jews were limited, he joined the family fabric business. It was an enterprise in which three generations worked together, my great-grandfather, my grandfather, my father and his brother Berl. It catered both to the public, and supplied smaller stores in and around Lachva.

My paternal grandfather, Sholom Romanowsky, would neglect his private affairs in favor of his philanthropic activities. Education and welfare were his primary concerns. He was deeply involved with the *Gemilut Chasodim*, the charity fund of our town, and sought to aid the needy in every way possible, and always with kindness. Grandpa kept a large, well-thumbed, grey marbleized hard cover ledger. In it he recorded the interest-free loans he extended and the purchases made from him on credit, always with the admonition to "pay whenever you can." To him, part of the value of giving was the manner in which it was done, to spare the recipient the shame of solicitation and the need to show gratitude. A pious man, he was the official *moehl* of Lachva. Grandpa Sholom performed all circumcisions solely for the *mitzvah*, the honor, never for gain. The general opinion of him was so high, that the rabbis called upon him to arbitrate disputes as an unofficial judge. The entire community was to each of us an extension of our own family. We lived together, we helped one another, and we shared our hopes and our ultimate dream of a new life in Palestine.

Friday is the day of the week which particularly stands out in my memory. It was mother's busiest day, because she was preparing for the coming of the Sabbath. While Hanka Tuchinsky, the maid, helped with the housekeeping chores, mother alone took care of the kitchen where there was fish and chicken to be cooked and *challah* and pastry to be baked. Father returned home before sundown to ready for the Sabbath eve services. We children were washed from head to toe, and dressed in our best outfits. Later we watched mother light the silver candelabra as she silently recited the blessing over the candles. Father usually brought a guest home for dinner, since strangers who found their way to our synagogue on a Friday night would customarily be invited for a Sabbath meal by one of the congregants. We waited for daddy to finish the blessing over the bread so we could start eating. After the meal we sang *zmirot* – songs of good cheer dedicated to the Sabbath, and we said grace. A sense of peace filled the house.

On Saturday, following morning services, we had *cholent* for lunch (potted meat and vegetables cooked on Friday and allowed to simmer overnight in the oven). It was kept warm from the previous day, since it is forbidden to start a fire on the Sabbath. Afterwards, the adults took their customary afternoon nap. When they reappeared, we children were sent to fetch mother's parents, Nechama and Yankl Rabinovitch, to visit for the remainder of the afternoon. We helped grandma with her heavy, fur-lined, coat which always had an aura of camphor about it, and, arm in arm we set out for our house. At home the steaming samovar stood in the center of the festive table. All drank tea, ate cake, cookies and fruit. My sisters and I entertained, we recited poems, sang songs and received much praise.

After evening prayers the family gathered at our great-grandfather Zeide Leibke Romanowsky's house to end the Sabbath with the traditional *Havdala* prayer. He lit the braided candle, and we all wished one another a good week – *a gute voch.*

Saturday was our only day of rest. On Sunday the Jewish community resumed its daily activities. Children went back to school where they were taught by extraordinarily dedicated teachers. Learning was held in the highest esteem. Everyone was literate in Yiddish and Hebrew, in addition to Polish and Russian. The community maintained a vital and flourishing spiritual life. It was progressive and vibrant, with organized lectures and a drama circle. A wide variety of Jewish books, newspapers and periodicals was readily available. Old traditions coexisted with a responsiveness to the modern world. Our Zionist organizations represented the whole range of Jewish political thought. The youth movements were particularly vital, and many emigrated to Palestine.

But the outside world was a hellish contradiction. Our *shtetl* Lachva, because of its geographic location between Russia and Poland, changed hands in time of war, with the Jews serving as scapegoats for both sides. The Poles of our region were viciously anti-Semitic. My grandparents often told how time and again Jews were the victims of *pogroms*. I remember always being afraid that some Poles would get drunk and attack Jews, as physical violence was not an uncommon occurrence. Yet, in spite of all tribulations, childhood for me was a very happy time.

Then came war, the Russians and the Nazis.

Suddenly it was 1939. Poland was partitioned by its neighbors, Germany and the USSR, and on September 17th Lachva was occupied by Russian troops. All organized Jewish activities came to a complete standstill. Our Hebrew school was closed, together with all other parochial schools, as a matter of government policy, and replaced with a general Russian language school. Few in the Jewish community were supportive of the new regime. The great majority were religious, and dedicated to Zionism. In the privacy of the home the Sabbath was kept, the Jewish holidays celebrated, and the Jewish identity retained. The new godless society had no real impact on our beliefs.

All private enterprise was confiscated as soon as the Soviet civil authorities assumed control, with token compensation made in worthless rubles. Children adapted best.

After the local dairy was shut down
Most families acquired a cow of their own.
A herder gathered the cattle each morning
And drove them to pasture.
At sunset, in a cloud of dust,
Sounds of moo, and the stench of manure,
The cows returned.
Marveling at how each cow knew
Just which yard to turn into,
We children sat on the stoop
Deciding that cows are really smart,
Unlike what grown-ups thought.
The milkmaid gave each of us a glass of milk,
Straight from the belly of the cow,
Still warm and covered with foam.
'Twas u d d e r l y wonderful!

Stringent travel restrictions were imposed. To visit friends in the next town, for example, an official travel permit had to be obtained. People were afraid to speak freely, lest some derogatory remark about the state land them in jail. Innocent comments were used against individuals to instill a feeling of guilt. There were newspaper reports of jailed parents turned in for disloyalty by their own children who, in turn, were praised for placing country above family. There were always informers, and no one ever knew who they were.

Purchases of goods not consistent with the buyer's official income could result in arrest and imprisonment on the theory that these had to be financed through black market activity. Nor was it beyond the Soviets to drum up false charges against those whom they wished removed from the community. You couldn't believe or trust anyone. Shortly our jails were full, and the courts were without justice. It was said that prisoners had scratched on the walls of the jail the phrase "Whoever hasn't been here, will be, and whoever has been, will not forget it."

In spite of the new restrictions placed on us, the Jewish population of Lachva grew due to an influx of refugees from German-occupied western Poland.

Life in our home was much subdued. The new leadership had relegated us to the lowest wrung of society, because we had been shopkeepers and not members of the working class. Our house was searched repeatedly, as were the homes of others under suspicion, and whatever the NKVD (later KGB, secret police) considered to be in over supply was simply confiscated. Worst of all were the *chistkas*. The word means cleansings, and referred to the periodic purges which took place. Undesirables, Jews and non-Jews alike, were sent to Siberia. The threat of being deported for the crime of having been shopkeepers was ever present. Our family slept in their clothing, and each of us had a knapsack packed and ready to grab whenever the expected knock on the door would come in the night. And come it would, for we had discovered that we were marked for deportation to Siberia. During this period the following story made the rounds: One man asks another, "What is happiness?" "When there is a knock on your door in the night," the other replied, "and the voice in the dark says 'Ivanov, come with me,' and you can say 'sorry, Ivanov lives in the apartment above,' that is happiness."

Because Jews were forbidden to own land, our population consisted largely of skilled artisans: tailors, shoemakers, blacksmiths and carpenters who continued to work at their crafts. Many of the former small shopkeepers, however, became bookkeepers for the various official Soviet trade unions. Thus, my father became the bookkeeper of the carpenter's cooperative, while my uncle occupied a similar position for a cooperative in an adjacent town. In this connection I remember an incident most vividly. After my father began to study bookkeeping, we had come to visit my great-grandparents who by this time were nearing ninety. As we stood by the window to watch them for a moment before entering their house, we observed great-grandfather speaking into his wife's "good" ear, explaining a passage from the bible. Whereupon my five-year old sister exclaimed: "Oh, grandpa is teaching grandma bookkeeping!" Why else would anyone pore so seriously over a book?

When the children in my class were about to be sworn into the Pioneers, the children's organization of the Communist Party, I was asked to leave the room. I was not accepted because of my family background. By this time I was a third grader in elementary school, and I felt terribly hurt to be one of the very few who could not wear the beautiful red scarf, held in place by a hammer and sickle clasp, like the rest of my classmates. But I did respond enthusiastically to the learning of the Russian language, poetry and music. All of the songs and poems taught us were in praise of Communism, of Lenin and of Stalin. Ironically, it fell to me to sing and recite these at our school and town functions, as I loved to perform and was the school's star performer.

The population in Russian-occupied Poland was kept in the dark about events beyond the borders. No publicity was given to the Nazi assault on Jewish life in areas occupied by the Germans. There was no criticism of Nazi Germany in the Soviet press. There was criticism only of a weak and backward Poland, from which we had been rescued.

And so we lived until June 22, 1941, when Germany suddenly invaded Russia. On July 8th Lachva fell to the advancing German armies. The Russians had retreated several days earlier, and our town was left in a state of total anarchy. No longer constrained by law and order, the most ignorant *muzhiks* (peasants) became a deadly threat to the Jewish population. They blamed us for all their troubles, and beating Jews and cutting off their beards became the order of the day. During that time a bunch of hooligans spotted an elderly Jew on the outskirts of town, and began to abuse and to beat him severely. They shouted "you dirty Jew, you killed Christ." When, in desperation, the old man exclaimed, "I swear it wasn't me, it must have been another Jew," they let him go...

Doors and shutters of Jewish homes were locked tightly, and we were afraid to venture out into the street. Inside homes fathers slept with axes under their pillows. My family paid a friendly neighbor, Stepan Tuchinsky, to help guard us at night.

It was almost with a sense of relief that we watched German troops on motorcycles roll through Lachva. My parents remembered the Germans from the time of the First World War as civilized, and hoped that they would reestablish some semblance of law and order.

They did establish order, but of what kind? Their order wreaked unbearable havoc on our lives. Persecutions began at once. They erected a bulletin board in the center of town on which they promptly began to post edict after edict. Every Jew was forced to wear a yellow round patch (instead of a Star of David), and to walk in the gutter only. Systematically, we were given deadlines for the surrender of our possessions, down to the sheets on our beds. Leaders of our Jewish community were arrested and held hostage to assure compliance with every German whim, and every order for the surrender of more and more of our belongings. This was always done under the threat of being searched. Should any of the confiscated items be found after the date set for their surrender, the hostages would be shot. We felt responsible for each other, and heeded every command. We still thought that if we cooperate, we'll survive. We didn't think of death and dying. Murder was inconceivable.

On August 13, 1941 the decree on the bulletin board called for all Jewish males to report at 4:00 a.m. the next morning to a designated spot on the edge of town, in order to be processed for work. That night some of our men were summoned, at gun point, to dig what was to be their own mass grave. The Nazis always disguised their motives. They had planned to kill them all. At dawn, on August 14th, aided by local collaborators, they drove all men from their homes shouting *heraus, schnell – out, fast!* My sisters and I clung to our father. We wanted to hide him away somewhere. Soon, we heard the heavy tread of boots on our steps, and father was taken from us.

In Lachva, as in other communities with Jewish populations, the Germans had appointed a governing body, or *Judenrat*, consisting of members of the Jewish community, through whom they exercised their authority. The head of our *Judenrat* was Dov Lopatin, a most able and dedicated leader, who did all he could to protect his fellow Jews. That morning he ran to SS headquarters to plead our cause. He convinced the Germans that they stood to benefit from retaining our Jewish men as a labor pool to be utilized locally. A reprieve was granted. Neighboring Jewish communities were not equally fortunate. Within days news reached us of the murder of their men.

The SS unit which had been sent to Lachva for the purpose of killing our men was quartered in the homes of local peasants. My father was one of a group sent to a farmyard where German horses were stabled. His job that day was to brush the horses' hides until they shone. I chanced to see father's back that evening, as my mother applied what remedies there were. It was crisscrossed with bruises and sores from repeated whip lashings. He told how German officers called each man in turn to submerge his head into a barrel of water. This amused them and made them laugh. Later, one SS man, when he could not be overheard, whispered cautiously to my father: "If I were a Jew, I'd kill myself." That, in my father's eyes, made him a "good" German.

Obsessed with fear, I spent every moment of each day on the look-out. Through the spaces between the slots of the shutters in my parents' bedroom window, I was able to see far down our street which led to the police station. I would get up at dawn to begin my watch, and remain there until it was too dark to see. Riveted to that spot, I kept repeating the prayer *Shema Yisroel* as well as the two passages from Psalms which grandpa Sholom gave me, assuring me that it would help, and that God would save us from evil.

One day I spotted the massive frame of our *Bürgermeister* Gretchko, the newly appointed mayor, together with his cohorts, marching up our street. Immediately, I alerted my parents. Before long there came a knock at our door. It seems Gretchko had been looking for a place to live, and was free to select any Jewish home of his choice. Our house, and everything in it, suited him best. Within days we had to leave. We took only some articles of clothing, and I carried my favorite winter coat.

We moved in with relatives, the Bukchin family, who let us use the upper story of their small one-family house. It fell within the perimeter of the ghetto, soon to be established.

On Passover eve, April l, 1942, the Jews of Lachva were herded into the newly formed ghetto, and were not permitted to bring any of their remaining possessions with them. The few Jewish families of Mokrove and Sinkewicz were also brought to the Lachva ghetto, since there were not enough of them to form a separate ghetto. Our ghetto was located in a Jewish section of town, which had been enclosed with barbed wire. On the east it was bordered by the River Smertz, and it was divided into two unequal parts by a road leading to a bridge crossing this river. Communications between the two parts of the ghetto were permitted briefly every day, the road remaining open to civilian and military traffic the rest of the time. I lived with my family in the larger part of the ghetto. Its only entrance was a huge iron gate which faced the *mark*, the market square.

There were upward of forty-five people living in each of the forty or so ghetto houses under the most intolerable conditions. The severe overcrowding greatly aggravated the ever worsening problems of disease and starvation. Every morning all "able" men and women were marched off to work. They drained swamps and repaired roads. The younger children remained in the ghetto, where, for example, they spent time unraveling old sweaters and turning them back into balls of yarn. This was then used to knit, utilizing a looser stitch, new articles of clothing – mittens, socks and sweaters – in anticipation of the coming winter. This gave the children some sense of purpose. At night the Nazis counted heads in the ghetto under the threat that if anyone were missing, many would be shot. None attempted to escape. There were always hostages taken from our most noted citizenry, and one of my parents was generally included. Once, on a very sunny day, I sneaked up to the iron doors of the dark little corner building where my mother was being held with other women. How I wept when she finally recognized my voice, and I heard her ask for the time and whether it was night or day.

Our spirits fell steadily. We grew thin and pale on our starvation rations. The horror of impending death and destruction mounted. Our three wooden synagogues, all of which fell within the ghetto, were filled as we prayed for a miracle.

By the beginning of September 1942, conditions had become unbearably harsh. Stripped of all our belongings, worn out by hunger and forced labor, and exhausted from the struggle to survive, we could not make it through the torments of another winter. The consequences of our ever worsening plight were dehumanizing. Rumors of the destruction of entire Jewish communities abounded. The Germans were not to be appeased, except by the flesh and blood of our people. We prayed for life. *God have mercy upon us! Where are you? Why do you keep silent and let this happen?*

In the hour of our greatest need, there, where we had lived for generations as devout Jews, there was no God to hear his people's cry. In vain had we placed our trust in Him. The whole world had kept its silence. There was neither divine nor human response to our anguished plight. Abandoned, we were doomed.

With the arrival of the *Einsatzgruppe,* the liquidation unit, on September 2nd, 1942, security around the ghetto was tightened. We knew that our time had run out. Just a little over a year ago Dov Lopatin had negotiated with the Germans and obtained the release of our men. Now we could only cling to the hope that he could repeat this miracle. But this time his pleas were of no avail. When he returned from SS headquarters he could only say "Nothing will move them. Each one of you do what you can to escape."

Our young people, the kind who are born old, had secretly begun to lay the groundwork for an uprising from the very first day of the ghetto's existence. They met throughout under the guidance of Yitzhak Rokchin. All attempts to procure firearms failed, but they were able to arm themselves with axes and iron bars. One group was assigned to set the ghetto aflame should the end come. They secretly accumulated kerosene and naphtha for this purpose. Our rabbis and pious Jews, in their unwavering faith, opposed an uprising, believing that we must leave ourselves to the will of the Divine.

Many young people would have attempted escape, but out of their deepest concern for the women, children and elderly, they stayed. Digging out their meager store of weapons, they stood ready to take on the might of the German forces.

On September 3, 1942, early in the morning, German troops carrying machine guns entered the ghetto and ordered us out of our houses, and to line up four abreast. Their plan was to march us in orderly fashion to open ditches, and shoot us. Lopatin poured kerosene over the house where the *Judenrat* had functioned and set fire to it as a signal to our resistance fighters to take action. Then our boys poured kerosene over the other ghetto houses and set them on fire. The Nazis panicked and began shooting at random into the hysterical mob. As Yisroel Drepsky, the first victim, fell, Yitzhak Rokchin, ax in hand, split the skull of one of the soldiers before my very eyes. Pursued by a spray of bullets, he ran toward the river, where he fell dead. The other boys threw themselves at the Germans with their axes, killing eight of them. Chaos ensued. Flames engulfed the ghetto. Children were knocked down and trampled. People were falling all around as bullets struck them. The mob, as if with a mind of its own, swayed back and forth, as families struggled to hold on to one another. Finally, under the weight of this wall of hysterical humanity, the iron hinges of the ghetto gate gave way. We began spilling out into the open market square. All who could, ran. Separated from my family, I too was running under the hail of bullets and jumping over bodies as they fell and lay sprawled all about me. I ran with all my might across the market place, through the streets of Lachva, and into the fields beyond, until I reached the outlying forest.

I looked back, terrified. The sky over my beloved *shtetl* was ablaze. At that moment of supreme anguish, and for the first time in my life, I became conscious of myself as being separate from my parents. It was possible for them to die, and for me to live. Exhausted, I took a deep breath to be sure that I was really alive, and from fright and horror sank onto a tree stump to wait. For what? I didn't know. Had anyone else made it this far?

Some men did pass by, but they were not about to pick up someone else's twelve-year-old when they had just lost their own families and did not know what lay before them. I felt sure that the Germans and their collaborators among the peasants would pursue the escapees. Suddenly, there was a stir in the bushes. I didn't move. With my heart barely contained, I saw Nioma, a boy from Lachva, holding my eight-year-old sister's hand, and then my father on the other side of her. We fell on one another...

Father told me that in the confusion of the uprising he had become separated from my mother, Menia, 36, and my older sister, Esther, 16.

The Jewish uprising in Lachva was the first revolt of a Polish ghetto [that resulted in German fatalities], according to H. A. Michaeli's *First Ghetto to Revolt – Lachva: Memorial Library of Jewish Communities*. Jerusalem, 1957, (in Hebrew). Facing imminent defeat, our boys fought heroically to the end. In the confusion, some 90 out of the 2,000 Jews in the ghetto escaped. Between six and seven hundred lost their lives during the fighting. The Germans then marched the others – the elderly, young children, religious Jews who would not flee – to an open ditch, had them undress, then shot and buried them in a mass grave near the burning ruin of what had once been our town. For days after, the grave kept rising and falling, as many had been buried while still alive.

Ours was one of only three ghetto families in which as many as three members survived the uprising. We never stopped wondering how the world could still be here after it had ended in the ghetto that morning.

Having escaped our ghetto and the German bullets, a small group of us crossed the forest outside Lachva and entered the Pripet Marshes beyond, where we roamed the rest of the day. Suddenly we heard voices and saw the ruddy faces of the soldiers of a German SS patrol led by local collaborators. They were searching for escaped Jews. We lay hidden, motionless, in the underbrush near a fork in the path. The Germans halted briefly at the fork before continuing to their left away from us, and we remained undetected. A moment later they fired a blind volley of shots. Once again Providence had been with us.

It was a warm, Indian summer day. The sun seemed ready to shine forever. While running for our lives, we had thrown off much of our clothing and lost our shoes. The harvest had just been gathered and it took all our strength to walk onward across the fields of stubble that cut our feet. Father took the shirt off his back, ripped it and tied the rags around my sister's and my feet. After sunset it suddenly grew cold. Frost covered the ground. I shivered all over, down to my bare feet. I stuffed hay under my sweater for warmth. It was our first night away from home.

Hungry and cold, we crawled under a huge haystack. I fell asleep, but was awakened by men arguing in whispers. I heard one of them say to my father, "We are going to sneak away from all these kids. We'll never make it alive with them. Leave your children and come with us!" I listened with my heart in my mouth, and I heard my father's firm "NEVER." When we awoke at dawn, the men were gone. They were the town's fisherman and Yankl Mester, a timber merchant, who knew these marshes well. We later learned that they were caught the next day and shot on the spot.

Our group now included my father, my sister and me; frail and frightened Zelik the tailor – the only other man who stayed; Sara, a young woman, and distant relative; cousin Itche Fishman; and several children ranging in age from 8 to 14. Our aim was to head eastward toward the Russian lines, and we spent the next day winding our way toward the Pripet River. We spotted some object on the far bank. At dusk, Itche, 16, who later perished during a partisan action, swam the river and brought a small fishing boat to us. It could not hold all of us at once. The children were afraid that my father would abandon them if he were to cross the river successfully with his own girls. They insisted that one of us be on the second crossing. And so it was. It took two trips, and most of the night, to make it across. With the wind blowing the boat off course and German motor boats controlling the river, each group, as it departed, feared it would never see the other again. But the boat ferried us all safely to the other side.

Once on the opposite shore of the Pripet River, we headed for the home of Kirush, a farmer my father knew well. His family, members of the landed gentry, had been customers at our fabric store for over a generation. Frightened, Kirush made the sign of the cross and would not let us enter, but took us to a hiding place in a densely wooded area some distance from his farm. Every night we waited for him to bring us bread and news of the whereabouts of Russian partisan camps. The children watched closely to make sure that father distributed the bread equitably. Each portion was enough for two or three bites. Those with greater self-control took a tiny bite and wrapped the rest in a large leaf for later. We quenched our thirst with the dew that gathered on the leaves toward morning. At night we were covered with goose bumps. Kind Zelik gathered the children around him, holding a couple at a time within his arms. Sometimes he would lie on top of a trembling child to warm and comfort him.

We could not remain hidden for long in territories dominated by the Germans. Our only chance for survival depended on reaching an area controlled by Russian partisans. At great risk, Kirush concealed us for eight or nine days while he looked for a trustworthy guide to take us to the Grichin Marshes, a vast wilderness we had to cross to reach underground territory. All night we walked in single file, following in the footsteps of our guide. At a predetermined destination, he left us. My father carried with him some money he had taken out of hiding that last morning in the ghetto, thinking he might need it to bribe his way to life. He gave all of it to Kirush and to our guide, with promises of additional reward to Kirush after the war. But Kirush was shot by the Russians as they reconquered the area shortly before the end of the war.

We continued to walk eastward for weeks, oblivious to time and distance, in the hope of crossing over to the Russian side, but had to give up. The war was going well for the Germans, who were advancing on all fronts. We decided to remain in the forest since further attempts to reach the front were hopeless. Russian troops cut off from the front became the partisans at whose side we hoped to outlast the war. We met other Jews who were in hiding. Some children in our group were reunited with friends or relatives. As they left us, they said that they owed their lives to my father. One of the luckiest was Feigele Gitelman, who had been hit by a German bullet while fleeing. She found her father.

Far from home, we slept in the woods on the outskirts of villages. We lived on what we could beg. Every day we had to find something to eat, and we were concerned entirely with obtaining food. We conducted practice sessions: "Dear lady, please help a starving child. God will surely reward you." Then we went out into the street. The kinder peasants would say, "You should have died with your parents, this is no life for kids."

Not only did we learn to beg, we learned to steal. We would sneak up to the most distant corner of a field in the dark of night, dig up potatoes and run back as fast as we could, lest dogs be set on us.

When we heard of the Russian Orthodox custom of placing food on family graves at Easter, we conducted "operation cemetery." My sister and I shared the hard boiled egg that was my father's booty. When the peasants called the disappearance of the food "a miracle" that morning, we listened without a word, but not without a pang of conscience.

Our group now numbered eleven, including five children. We built a little log cabin in the woods, camouflaged under twigs and branches, with the help of a poor, kind farmer, Stepanetchko, in exchange for a promise of a reward after the war. We could sit or lie in the hut, but there was no room to stand. We had a fire going all the time in the center of the cabin, and there were almost always potatoes to bake. We kept continuous watch over the fire, fanning the embers lest they go out completely. Then, one bitterly cold night, a spark jumped to the cabin logs. Father attempted to extinguish the spark with a stick. Instead, his effort fanned the spark and the entire structure was consumed by fire like a bale of straw. We walked, under a full moon, through deep snow, for about two miles to find shelter with Hershele, who had his own flimsy structure built for four. Now it had to hold eleven more. We all piled into the small space, literally stacked one on top of the other. Within days we began to build a new cabin, again with the help of Stepanetchko.

We measured time by the sun and the seasons, and found our bearing by the stars at night. The chaos of war did not interfere with the orderliness of nature. We were always on the lookout for danger. A peasant could betray us, and partisans were known to have killed many a Jew. I shudder to recall the fate of Nioma, the young man who fled the ghetto with my father and little sister. He was shot by a commander of the Russian underground. The official reason for the execution: "The Jew was caught dozing on guard." Everyone knew the true reason: the commander coveted Nioma's eyeglasses.

But our greatest fear was being caught by the Germans. Periodically, they swept through the hinterland villages on "roundup" (or "cleansing") missions. Peasants were killed, cattle slaughtered, farms destroyed. We trusted no one and constantly changed our location lest someone report us to the Germans. In the wintertime we were particularly afraid of discovery, because of the tracks we left in the snow. We felt safe only when fresh snowfall obliterated them.

The worst of roundups occurred in the winter of 1942-1943. We fled our cabin under cover of night and trekked through virgin forest, through undergrowth that scratched and bruised us. We walked single file as we followed in the leader's, Leibl Slutzky's, steps in order to leave only one set of footprints. With hearts thumping, my sister and I concentrated on making the extra long steps in the tracks of the adults. The snow was knee deep and it was difficult to pull my foot out after each step. Having walked for some hours, we took shelter in an abandoned shack. The next morning there came a shout: "The Germans are coming." Instantly we faded into the wilderness. The Germans had entered the woods on skis. Moments after we left, they passed the shack and demolished it with a grenade.

The sweep lasted several days. After it ended, we returned to look for our good friend, Stepanetchko. Arriving in the midst of a steady whirl of snowflakes, we found him and his family brutally shot, his cattle killed and his meager farm burned to the ground. The Germans had suspected him of aiding and abetting the partisans. A similar fate befell all farmers in the area.

Among the ruins of Stepanetchko's farm we found his ax and small saw, both damaged by fire, which we used to prepare firewood. Thereafter, we searched the wreckage of other farms which had been destroyed, looking for anything usable.

All eleven of us kept close together. Whenever the wind rattled the trees, we looked around apprehensively. We listened and speculated on the origin of every sound, from the loud noise of a falling tree to the snapping of a twig.

Survival was our all-consuming concern. But at night, under cover of darkness, hidden behind thick curtains of trees, we often could relax a little and sing. Only the howling of wolves would stop us. Each of us taught the others the prayers and songs he knew, until we all had an extensive repertory in several languages. Our favorite was a popular Yiddish song, *Zol Shoyn Kumen Di Ge'uleh,* in which we questioned our Messiah. Where was He, and why was He waiting so long? With our bellies empty, we concocted the most marvelous recipes, paying special attention to spices.

In the woods we were captive and free at the same time. We had little food but the air made us feel alive. I listened to the wild birds and other animals, loved the feel of the earth in the spring and the sweet scent of blossoms.

"Are there still places on earth where children play, where they get up in the morning, eat breakfast, go to school and are not afraid?" I'd ask. Inevitably one of our optimists would reply, "I can just imagine you all grown up, wearing silk stockings, shiny patent leather, high heel shoes and a feather in your hat." Everyone laughed.

Week followed week and season merged into season. Finally, one day our partisan friends gave us some very good news. "The Russians are repelling the Germans, and if you put your ears to the ground, and listen carefully, you may hear the rumbling of the front." This we did at night, when sounds could best be distinguished. At first we heard distant thuds, then strong booms rolled underground. Sometimes there were no sounds at all. One day a peasant on horseback rode by and said, "The Russian army is marching through the village of Berezniak. Tired and dirty soldiers are sharing their bread with everyone." We were liberated and didn't even know it. The Germans retreated so rapidly that there was no fighting in our immediate area. The war was over for us and we were alive and free. It was July of 1944.

Through our two years in the woods, our narrow escapes and our ever present hunger, we never cried. Suffering from cold and from want, dressed in rags, excluded from human society, we still clung to hope. And now we were going home to look for other survivors who might have lived through the war years. "Maybe my mother..." I dared say to myself. I bargained with the Almighty. "Dear God, if there are others, my faith in You will be restored." Everyone grew tense as we approached Lachva.

Most of the town no longer existed. In its place was a field where carrots grew. We sought out the lot where our house once had stood, and found our garden overgrown with weeds. There I was, skin and bones and old beyond my years, under our weeping willow tree where I had stood a thousand times as a little girl. My tears flowed freely.

We ran to find our Christian friends and neighbors among the peasants whose houses remained standing. At first they backed away from us as if we had risen from the dead, but soon began to name those of our family and those of our friends whom they had seen dead. We wept inconsolably as they listed name after name. That night I tried to pray again, but my heart wasn't in it. Why did God allow fellow humans to rob me of my faith in Him? I felt intolerable loss. I visited the mass grave of our Jewish martyrs every day. I felt that I was living for them also. Those who did not survive must be remembered. I became conscious of a deepening of my capacity to feel.

Little sour green apples grew in abundance in Lachva. After years of eating almost nothing but saltless potatoes, we ate these apples ravenously and were stricken with dysentery. My case was severe. Every day my father lifted me into a sitting position, placed himself against my fragile frame to support it, and fed me the soup he had made from bones and vegetables he had begged. Though I had no appetite at all, we both knew that I had to force some down... He nursed me night and day, and in time I began to show signs of improvement. The day came when he held me up and helped me across the room. A mirror hung diagonally on one wall. I caught a glance of myself: a face drained of color, sunken cheeks, dry lips, sad eyes. I looked like a shadow, more dead than alive. I cried at the image in the mirror and my father stood beside me, also weeping. His reflection in the corner of that mirror became fixed forever in my mind.

My father was determined for us to leave this bloody Europe before the Russians reestablished firm control and made it impossible to flee. But we had to remain in Lachva for some months before we were able to leave, and very painful months they were.

We decided to make our way toward the part of Europe occupied by Western allies, and reached Föhrenwald, a displaced persons camp in Germany, where we remained for seven months. We wanted to go to Palestine but because of the British mandate, entry was denied us. Before the war, my father had addressed the letters that his parents and grandparents wrote to our kin in America. Miraculously he remembered their address and wrote to them after the war. He told them that out of our entire family, only the three of us and his brother Berel's daughter, Lea, survived. Our American relatives sent us visas for the United States. Lea subsequently made her way to Palestine via Italy.

On May 24, 1946, we arrived in New York. At first we were deluged by visitors flocking to hear news of their own families. There was much noise in Tante Peshe's house in the Bronx. Then the visitors stopped coming and we entered that special loneliness of survivors when they attempt to rejoin normal life. My father's cousin and her husband, "Aunt" Betty and "Uncle" Joe, took special interest in our welfare and that helped a lot.

My sleep was constantly interrupted by nightmares. We were destitute and father did not know how to provide for us. The owner of a neighborhood fabric store hired him as a favor, but the pay was very low.

Happily, our state of poverty did not prevent me from attending school. Having been denied all formal schooling from 1940 to 1946, I had a consuming ambition to obtain an education. After all, I had seen material possessions confiscated in an instant, but your mind cannot be taken from you. The task I set myself was to become educated.

Within two years I completed high school, and subsequently attended the evening session at Hunter College. After graduating with a B.A. in Russian, I taught at Stuyvesant High School in New York. In 1966 I received an M.A. degree from New York University. Through the years, I immersed myself in poetry and music, made many friends and received much flattery from men. I married and I had two daughters.

In spite of a busy new life, I never filled the gap created by the loss of everything I loved and believed in – my family, my people, my God. I live in two different worlds and each new experience evokes images from the past. I walk in the park and suddenly I am eight years old walking in the fields of Lachva with my mother. Each time I think of Lachva, and I think of it every day, I remember death in the ghetto that September morning.

I cannot help but live in the grip of my Holocaust experiences.

After the defeat of Germany, the units and the individuals responsible for the murder of the Jews of Lachva and surrounding communities were identified. Based on material furnished by the Soviet Union to the prosecution in West Germany in 1963, an investigation was started against 18 Nazi criminals who took part in the killing actions against the Jews of Pinsk district during the period of August – November 1942. All of them were released on 10-25,000 DM bail until the trial. The trial took place in Frankfurt am Main, and lasted from November 25, 1971 to February 6, 1973.

The following information and excerpts from testimony gathered in Germany and Israel was used during the trial in Germany. This, as well as additional information obtained from the Yad Vashem archives in Jerusalem, and other sources, was collected by Joshua Lior-Lichtstein, who resides in Israel, and holds a Master of Arts degree in Jewish History. He is a survivor of Lachva ghetto, and appeared as a witness.

The fate of the Lachva Jewish community was described in these sources as follows:

The ghetto in the provincial town of Lachva with a predominantly Jewish population, which is situated to the east of Pinsk, along the railroad line Brest-Gomel, was established the end of March or beginning of April, 1942. In Lachva the Jewish men were spared from the killing actions in 1941, during which time Jewish men from age 18 to 60 in surrounding Jewish communities were shot by members of a special unit.

The ghetto consisted of 45 to 50 houses with somewhat more than 2,000 inhabitants.

Living conditions were pitifully poor. The overcrowding was

unbearable. Very often three to four families had to share one room. There was hardly any food. The people in the ghetto were soon run down and neglected. Their bellies were swollen from hunger, they suffered from starvation edema and had no clothing. No Jew was allowed to leave the ghetto without the permission of the German authorities. Violators were to be shot on the spot.

On September 3, 1942 the Lachva ghetto was destroyed on orders from the SD (Sicherheitsdienst) headquarters in Rowno. The order was carried out under the direction of the leader of the SD office in Pinsk, the late witness Rasp, who was also in charge at the site of the open execution pit.

Rasp, the SD commander in Pinsk, had received an order from SS State Security Headquarters in Berlin, that during the period from August to the beginning of November, 1942, all ghetto Jews in the Pinsk district are to be liquidated. Preliminary instructions were as follows:

1. To organize the preparation and digging of the Erschiessungsgruben (execution pits) for the Jews.

2. To close the exit from the ghetto by securing the fences and gates, and by increasing the number of guards.

3. To concentrate the ghetto Jews in one place and escort them to the ditches with assistance from the Ukrainian militia and German gendarmerie.

4. The ghetto to be surrounded in the morning hours, and to be completely cleared of Jews.

5. The Jews to be escorted by armed troops to the execution pits in marching columns of 100 persons each. The assembly place in the ghetto to be under strict guard.

6. Near the pits the Jews to be formed in a line, forced to lie with face to the ground, and be killed by shooting.

7. Those following should lie on those killed, and be shot.

8. Prior to the killing action, and subsequent to it, the security people and all other participants to receive vodka.

Just before the action, the killers received the following instructions:

1. Those assigned to searching the ghetto for hidden Jews in

order to round them up for the killing action, are to be equipped with axes and other tools in order to break into houses where Jews may be in hiding.

2.   All attics to be thoroughly searched for Jews who may be hiding in them.

3.   All basements and bunkers should be checked with the help of bloodhounds, or by throwing hand grenades into them forcing the Jews to come out.

4.   The areas adjacent to the houses to be probed with sharp iron rods to search for Jews who may be hiding underground.

The clearing of the Lachva ghetto started around 9:00 o'clock after the SD Kommando Unit Pinsk, which on the way shot the Jews in the village of Kozangorodok, seven kilometers away, had arrived under the command of the witness Rasp. The Jews were taken from their houses and driven onto an open street in the ghetto. The Jews in the Lachva ghetto had already heard of the destruction of the neighboring ghettos of Mikashewicze and Lenin. It also had become known that under the direction of the local authorities, ditches had been dug alongside the railroad tracks.

The young men of Lachva decided, therefore, "not to let themselves be slaughtered like cattle" as the surviving witness Leon Slutzky explained, "but to defend themselves." The chairman of the *Judenrat* set fire to the house of the *Judenrat* as a prearranged signal for the uprising to begin. The ghetto was now set on fire from all sides. The Jews defended themselves with firearms and hand grenades of their own making, in an attempt to break through the ghetto gates and to escape. This provoked panic in the crowd of people who had been driven out into the open.

As a result of the uprising 500 to 600 Jews, mainly men, managed to escape from the ghetto. The guards shot machine gun and rifle fire indiscriminantly at the fleeing Jews and into the crowd. Some 800 people lost their lives in the fire and by shooting. The remaining group of some 600, mainly old people, women and children, surrendered. They were driven to the pit, some 1 1/2 kilometers from the ghetto. The pit was 25 meters long, 2 meters wide and 2 1/2 meters deep. About 20 to 30 meters before reaching the ditch they had to undress. From this spot the shootings at the ditch were clearly visible. Many Jews refused to walk voluntarily into the ditch. They were driven by force in groups of five. Once there, they had to lie face down on the ground or, later, on those already shot. With the exception of one physician, Dr. Igelnik, who was spared after reaching the ditch, at least 500 were shot.*

Of the 500 to 600 Jews who escaped the ghetto, at least 350 were caught by mounted troops and police who hunted them down and shot them on the spot. About 120 Jews of the ghetto survived the massacre.

Precise information reached Pinsk headquarters concerning the revolt of Lachva Jews, who actually succeeded in killing several Germans. Confirmation of the armed resistance in Lachva was substantiated by the Vice-Kommissar Alfred Ebner, who boasted to have annihilated all Jews of the surrounding areas because of that revolt.

The accused Petsch, member of the SD Kommando Pinsk, acted mainly as executioner at the pit. With a Russian-made machine pistol he killed men, women and children with a single shot in the neck from a distance of about 50 cm. From time to time, Balbach and Patik relieved him. At those times he helped drive the remaining victims to the ditch. During the action small amounts of alcohol were distributed to the SD men. At about 4:00 o'clock in the afternoon the action was completed and from then on larger amounts of alcohol were distributed.

The witness Helde, who, as guard, helped to drive the Jews to the ditch, was struck by the behavior of the SD men. They tried to calm the Jews by telling them that they would kill them as quickly and painlessly as possible. At his interrogation, the witness Kappe said that the recollections of a young Jewish girl of about 13 or 14 years of age was burned into his memory. She was not

---

*Author's note: Dr. Shlomo Igelnik was killed when he refused to treat the wounded Nazi soldiers. He came to Lachva in 1939, a refugee fleeing Nazi occupied western Poland.

killed immediately by the shot in the neck, and, bleeding, staggered over the dead bodies until an SD man gave her the coup de grace.

During the Nazi period the German judicial system was subservient to the state, and justice did not exist. Following defeat of World War ll, Germany adopted a very liberal legal system, and the death penalty was abolished.

The following is a brief description of how the accused fared before the bar of German justice, again taken from the material gathered by Joshua Lior-Lichtstein:

ADOLF PETSCH – born in 1915, in Kronitz, in the Sudetenland. Participated in driving Jews to the pits and shooting men, women and children to death with a shot in the neck with a machine pistol. Took part in the murder of the following numbers of victims:

Town	# Jews killed
Lachva	500
Luninec	2,800
Wisotzk	1,400
Davidhorodok	1,100
Stolin	6,500
Janow	1,500

Adolph Petsch was given a sentence of only 15 years imprisonment.

HEINRICH WILHELM PLANTIUS – born in 1914, in Frankfurt. Accused of taking part in the murder of 16,200 Jews. After the war he was employed by the Frankfurt municipality, and belonged to the Evangelical Church. Following the trial he was sentenced to four years imprisonment.

JOHAN JOSEF KUHR – born in 1916 and lived in Frankfurt. Became a police official in Frankfurt in 1954. Accused of participating in the murder of at least 16,200 Jews. He was sentenced to two-and-a-half years imprisonment.

HEINZ DIETER TELTZ – born in 1916, in Wiesbaden. Took part in the murder of Jews, and was in command of the killing actions in Stolin, Janow, Lachva and Luninec. After the war he joined the police in Dusseldorf as Pollizeikommissar, eventually achieving the rank of *Polizeihauptkommissar*. Sentenced to three years' imprisonment.

RUDOLF KARK ECKERT – born in 1914, in Hamburg. Took part in killing actions against Jews in Biala Podlaska, Drohiczyn and Lachva. Noted for his brutality. After the war he served with the Hamburg police as *Polizeihauptkommissar*. Sentenced to three years imprisonment. He continued to receive a monthly pension of 1,000 German Marks.

WALTER HEINRICH KARL LEONHARD GROSS – born in 1911, in Frankfort. Took part in killing actions in Lublin, Pinsk, and all towns in the vicinity. After the war he served with the German police as *Polizeihauptwachmeister*. He was sentenced to four years imprisonment.

Observers found that the judges turned the trials into mockery. They released most of the accused, 12 out of 18, for "lack of evidence", and ruled that no one could be held accountable for the deaths of those Jews who were killed in the ghetto or while escaping from the ghetto during the Jewish revolt in Lachva. Much of the proceedings revolved around the number of Jews killed at the ditch, whether 500 or 600, for a lower number would provide an excuse for imposing lighter sentences. Thus the verdicts rendered.

Why I Write

I've been silent so long,
Now I'm obsessed.
Language is wanting,
But I must struggle
To put it in words.

I write to justify my survival
Summoned by the millions who died.
I write to testify,
To take the world, and God, to task
For their silence.
I write to search for answers,
For release and for repair,
Lest my grief spill over.

Lawlessness

Father kept an ax under his pillow,
Stepan Tutchinsky, a friendly neighbor,
Helped guard our house at night.
Bands of ignorant *muzhiks*
Beat Jews, cut off their beards,
Hurled rocks with inordinate vigor,
Yelling "you killed Christ!"

Shattered windows tightly shuttered,
Doors locked, bolted, barricaded.
The Russians withdrew,
The mob took over.
We waited for the Germans to arrive
And restore some civil order.

Finally, shots grew closer,
Motorcycles with sidecars
Advanced through town.
Then came ground troops
Stomping behind swastika flags,
Giving the Nazi salute...

German Invasion

Suddenly there was the German invasion.
Primitive fear mixed with rational thought:
"They're civilized people" our parents said.
And though they tried to keep a calm exterior
And even speak to us kids of cheerful things,
We sensed that they were worried,
And that made us afraid
And filled our minds with dark imaginings.
We gauged our circumstance
By their expressions.
When they smiled a little,
For that moment,
We were not afraid.

I felt secretly reassured
When, level with my child's eyes,
I saw the inscription
On the soldiers' belt buckles,
Gott Mit Uns – God's with us.
But why the *Hakenkreutz*, the Swastika?

In place of God, they worshipped murder,
Obsessed with genocide,
Devouring in cold blood
As many defenseless innocents
As they could,
Calling themselves
Honorable German soldiers.

Dear God, I expected better from you!

Gretchko

Muttering prayers, riveted
By that tightly shuttered window
Peering through the gaps between slots,
On constant guard.

One day I spotted Gretchko's
Massive frame, and over-fed face,
Advancing up our street with his horde.
As newly appointed *Bürgermeister*
The Nazis gave him choice
Of any Jewish home.
He selected ours.
"This suits me fine," he said, "get out at once,"
Baring his gold tooth as he grinned.

We took the few possessions allowed,
And I carried my favorite coat.
After a final look around the house they had built,
My parents carefully closed the door behind them,
And, we went...

Grandfather's Tears

The Germans issued their edict
To surrender our worldly belongings.
They took hostages,
Including our parents.

Grandfather came to comfort us:
"Keep your faith and trust in God" he said.
And we implored the Almighty in prayer
To bring our parents back.

Then grandpa raised his fragile hands
As if to place on us a blessing,
To bid us life itself, perhaps,
And we saw tears in grandpa's eyes.

The ghetto and destruction lay ahead.
My father, my little sister and I survived.
Grandfather perished with all the rest.

Grandfather died secure in his faith.
We go on in grief,
Questioning God's ways.

New Decrees

Day after day new decrees:
Wear yellow stars,
Walk only in the gutter,
Surrender all gold,
Then silver,
Furs and woolens,
Down to our linens.

Now their order
Called for all men,
Fourteen and over,
"Report at dawn, on the edge of town,
To be processed for work!"
Rifle butts pounded on every door,
Heraus! and *Schnell!*
Screaming for our boys and men,
The town half-wit among them,
Bewildered,
Led away by armed guards
In spotless uniforms
And shiny, black leather boots.

Dov Lopatin, head of our *Judenrat*,
Spurned their offer to be spared.
At SS headquarters he pled:
Let all men live
And continue as slave laborers.
The Nazis saw merit in his urging
And granted a reprieve.

"It fell to me" father said,
"To shine horses' hides,
When a "good German" whispered quietly:
"*Wenn ich ein Jude bin, wuerde ich Selbstmord begehen.*" –
"*If I were a Jew, I'd kill myself.*"

The soldiers now called each man in turn,
Submerged his head in a barrel of water
While they grew wild with laughter.

At night, with the kitchen door slightly ajar,
I saw father's back, a work of welts,
And mother washing his wounds.

No One Escaped

In the ghetto
After morning roll-call,
"Able" men and women,
Slaves in ragged clothes
Hanging on emaciated bones,
Were led off,
Four abreast,
To drain swamps
And build roads,
Under the scrutiny
Of merciless
SS and local guards.

At dusk, a column of ghosts,
Struggling to keep in step
To ward off rifle butt blows,
Came shuffling back.
Heads were counted once again
With their usual admonition:
"You will all be killed
If even one of you is missing!"

Each felt responsible
For the others' fate,
The numbers always checked,
No one escaped.

The Abandoned

Children in the Ghetto

Hemmed in alone in the ghetto,
We children would unravel old sweaters,
Reknit them in a looser stitch
To save some wool for socks,
A hat, or maybe mittens
In time for winter.

Or, we'd lie by the high
Barbed wire fence
In wait
To see a bird,
Or catch the buzz of a bee,
Mumbling,
"Nothing's like it used to be."

So we talked to the sky above
Where God himself resides.
"We want to be somewhere else,
Anywhere that isn't here.
There must be so much
Somewhere else
In the world."

By the time winter arrived,
Our town was *Judenfrei*.

Grandpa Escaped Murder

Liquidation units arrived,
SS-men surrounded the ghetto.
"This time there'll be no reprieve,
Do what you can to survive,"
Our spokesman, Dov Lopatin, announced.

Cousin Lea began to search for food,
Stuffed her mouth, chewed and chewed.
Others swallowed poison.
Families hugged,
And wailed aloud in prayer.
Our boys stood ready
With their secretly accumulated
Axes, hammers and naphtha
To take on the killing squads
And torch the ghetto houses.

On hearing that the end had come,
Grandpa Yankl lay down, and
D i e d.
Our two Rabbis rushed to him
Certain he was chosen by God
To be spared the common fate.
A host of bony hands
Lifted grandpa's body into the air,
Carried him away
To the wooden Chasidic *shtibl*
Where he had worshipped
Three times each day,
And where he was soon consumed
By the flames
Of the ghetto uprising.

Ghetto Uprising, 1942

That last September morning
Without a miracle from above
From His invisible being
Or from the world below
    Abandoned we were doomed
    Our ghetto was to be consumed

The sun rose blood-red that morning
Ever faithful to its course
Shamefully it kept on shining
While death was waiting at our doors
    That day of judgment
    Our fateful moment

Jews an uprising staging
Germans caught by surprise
Ghetto houses blazing
Eight Nazis axed
    Barbed wire stormed
    Few of us escaped

All visions were ending
Gone was all hope
Cruelty was raging
In unimaginable scope
    Goodbye, childhood dreams
    And times yet to be ➡

The chaos that morning
The murder of my kin

When torment meant living
Days cruel beyond words
With no time for grieving
While roaming the woods
    I often was heartened
    By the love they imparted

Their piercing screams
Recurring in my brain
    Time can never heal
    Such overwhelming pain

I See Germans Shooting

I see Germans shooting
And I see the slain
A bloody stampede
Children knocked down
T r a m p l e d
My baby cousins
Cheva, Friedka, Niusia and Dovik
A human tidal wave
Streaming toward the ghetto gate
Tearing it off its hinges
Spilling out over it
Into the open market square
Into SS machine gun fire
My mother and older sister are there
Then I don't see them any more

Father never let go
Of my little sister's hand
I ran by myself
Somehow
We took the same path
We met

Cheva (top)
and her sister Fridka (middle),
Gershon Rabinovitch's two children,

Niusia (bottom) with her mother Penia,
Shmuel-Ber Rabinovitch's wife.

Premonition of a Twelve-year-old

They burst into the ghetto to "liquidate."
Amid German orders to descend to the street,
Clutching the one warm coat I had saved,
Some crazy voice in my head
Kept repeating "you'll need it, you'll live."

Then the uprising came, obscuring that sound,
The whistling of bullets now drowned it out.
Randomly bodies were struck and lay sprawled,
Jumping over them, dumping my coat,
I ran well beyond town, smoke billowed above.

At night in the marshes
I stuffed hay in my sweater
Against piercing cold.

The Abandoned

No Shoes

Beneath a hail of bullets
Made it to the edge of town
Where harvests newly gathered
Left fields of coarsest stubble.

Just steps,
And our bare feet were bloody,
Knife-like the stubble attacked,
Shoes came off somewhere while running.

Tearing his shirt into pieces
Father tied our delicate feet,
The rags soon were shredded and bloodied
And gone the way of the shoes.

Cast upon fields of stubble,
Forsaken by God and by man,
Friends and family murdered,
Why so frantic to go on?

The Pripet Marshes*

At night, in the Pripet Marshes,
Concealed under a haystack,
Our fisherman and Yankl Mester,
The timber merchant,
Came upon us.

Too fearful to sleep,
I heard their muted voices urge father:
"Leave your kids
And steal away with us
For a chance to survive."
They knew these wetlands best,
One barged tree trunks down its network
Of winding rivers and canals,
The other cast his nets
Into the Pripet River.
I strained my racing mind to listen,
'Till I heard my father's
"N E V E R."

Roaming the desolate Pripet Marshes
The fisherman and the timberman
Were caught
By local Nazi collaborators,
And shot on the spot.

*The Pripet Marshes are the largest swamps on the European
continent. They lie in the thickly forested basin of the Pripet River
and cover an area of about 104,000 square miles. Densely
wooded and largely uninhabited, the region has supported a
diversified lumber industry.

The Abandoned

We Escaped

In our group
There was father, forty-four,
My sister was eight,
And I was twelve years old.
There was Zelik the tailor,
Fortyish and cowardly,
Sarah, twenty-seven, a distant relative,
Cousin Itche Fishman, sixteen,
And invincible (he thought),
And several children, twelve to fourteen.
Driven off by others,
They attached themselves to us,
Because, they reasoned,
With children of his own
Father wouldn't abandon them.

And so it was.

Hunted

Hunted, we had to cross the river*
That very night.
Under darkness of a vacant sky,
From the top of trackless cliffs,
Down, down we groped
Over rugged thickets and jagged rocks
To the water's edge.

The river,
Stagnant with water-logged tree trunks,
Spanned as wide as eyes could see.
"Children first" was heard, "one at a time!"
Naked little nimble feet
Staggered from trunk to trunk,
Terrified of losing balance...

The water-logged tree trunks
Sank and rose with every step.
Ripples upon ripples broke the still surface,
Swept and swayed, and bore ever onward,
Then washed against the shore, and ceased.

We made it across.
The river was again asleep.

*The river is one of the network of streams and rivers that splinter
off into many directions in the Pripet Marshes.

The Abandoned

Mosquitoes

A high pitched buzzing
Strikes your ear.
 Instantly you're under siege.
Millions surround you,
Puncture your skin,
Suck your blood,
Leave red bumps
Wherever they reach.

You itch, and you scratch
Compulsively, by reflex,
By some uncontrollable
Primal instinct.
You're in your lowest depths.
You tear your skin,
Endure bleeding and pain.

D e f e n s l e s s,
You try to turn your thoughts away,
Only to find yourself asking:
Why are mosquitoes attracted to me?

Honing their skill for millions of years
They're expert at getting their bloody meals.
What a feast we must be to them
In this swampy wilderness
Empty of humans! ➡

It's not as if we're just out
Here in the elements
Enjoying the outdoors.
We're fleeing the Nazis
And their collaborators...

If you ask me,
The Creator blundered.
Had He no other cares
Than to bring forth
Such pernicious little creatures
To live and to multiply?

Hope there is no Heaven
For these heartless parasites.

The Pripet River*

Winding our way toward the Pripet,
We had no means of crossing.
Itche Fishman volunteered
To swim across and explore
The far bank.
Using the dusk for cover,
He threw himself into the river.
Hours passed, long as years,
We lost all hope of seeing him.
When at last he did appear,
We could only lament
The boat he had found
Was too small
To hold us all at once.

The children, afraid
Father would abandon them
If he were to go first
With his two girls,
Insisted one of us
Be on the second crossing.

The first group departed
With father at the oars.
The "ark" plowed over the water,
And disappeared.
Twice he went.
The German patrolling motor boats
Did not discover us,
Nor did the wind blow us off course.
We all made it safely across.

*The Pripet River is a 500-mile-long navigable river in southern
Belarus and northwestern Ukraine that flows east through the
Pripet Marshes, then joins the Dnieper River.

Kirush

On the eastern shore of the Pripet
We made for the home of Kirush,
A long time customer
At our family fabric store.

Father tapped on his window,
Ashen, Kirush appeared,
Made the sign of the cross,
But wouldn't let us in
Lest prying eyes lurk in the night.
Immediately
He led us away from his farm,
Hid us amid twisted bushes and trees,
Promised to come nightly with bread
And with news
Of partisan whereabouts.

We trusted him.
There was no one else.
And, Kirush risked his life for us.

He kept us concealed for eight or nine days,
All the while searching for a trustworthy guide
To take us to the Gritchin Marshes,
A vast wilderness we had to cross
To reach partisan controlled woods.

The Abandoned

The children watched closely
Father should distribute the bread fairly.
Some ate their share right-away,
Others took one bite, and saved the rest
Wrapped in a leaf.
Long we chewed,
Delayed swallowing,
Quenched our thirst collecting dew
Formed on the leaves toward morning.

September nights are cold in Poland.
There is frost on the ground.
Covered with goose bumps
We lay together entwined.
Kind Zelik held a trembling child
In his arms,
And even lay on top of him
For comfort and warmth.

September nights are cold in Poland.

Fireflies

We came to a sudden stop
Waiting to sneak across
The heavily guarded road.

Fear stricken,
And trembling,
Somehow – I became aware
Of fireflies glowing around me.
"They're not afraid
To flicker in the dark
And give themselves away?"
I nudged my little sister
Next to me.

We wanted to hide,
Become invisible,
Change our color to green
And remain in the forest
U n d e t e c t a b l e.

Blitzkrieg

Inch by inch we plodded onward
Past prickly bushes,
Swamps and streams,
Begged for food,
Slept in open woods
Or abandoned, fallen barns,
Heading ever eastward
To reach safety
Behind the Russian lines.
But the Germans passed swiftly
Through *blitzkrieg* offensive.
We had to give up
And remain in the woods.

Exhausted, my little sister
Slipped to the ground:
"I can't any more," she said,
"You might as well go on
Without me."
Father took her on his back,
And with me by his side,
We trudged from farm
To isolated farm
In search of food,
And a place to hide.

June 22, 1941

The Germans bomb Kiev,
Break the non-aggression pact,
Overrun Poland,
Drive ever eastward,
Toward Moscow,
Before the Russian winter.

Soviet armies
Cut off from the front
Become the partisans
At whose side
We hope
To outlast the war.

We encounter solitary individuals,
Mostly adults,
But also children,
All alien beings,
Eyes wide with terror,
Roaming the woods,
Fleeing the Germans.

We regroup:
Zelik and the children
Go with others,
Feigele finds her father.
We become a group of eleven,
Ages eight to fifty,
Including five children.

Nioma

Having escaped death in the ghetto
Nioma fled into the woods.
Not yet twenty, burning with vengeance,
He joined the partisans.
Unarmed, he went with them
To carry out raids,
And when he returned, rifle in hand,
He was accepted into their ranks.

One night by the fire,
Deep within the Russian forest,
Far behind the German front,
Lucky men who had their glasses
Tried each other's spectacles.
Some were actually swapped.
Hands were clasped, and deals were struck.
The commander, too, participated.
Though he hadn't worn them before,
With Nioma's glasses
His vision cleared.

Soon rumors maligning Nioma
Began to be heard:
"The Jew was dozing on guard."
Pretending righteous indignation,
The commander assembled his men
To witness a malingerer's punishment.
An unsuspecting Nioma was ordered to walk ahead,
And then, the commander shot him in the back.

Everyone knew what had truly happened,
Though no one dared utter a sound.
The commander coveted Nioma's glasses,
And now he had them for his own.

Defying the Odds

We could have died of terror,
Or grief,
Or hunger,
Or typhus fever
From lice and filth.
We could have been poisoned
By stagnant marsh water
We scooped up
And drank from father's shoe,
Or mushrooms
Resembling the edible variety.

We could have died
From exposure
To the full force
Of the long Russian winter,
Or wolves eager for prey.
We could have been betrayed
To the Germans
By some trusted
Local peasant
Turned informer.

We didn't die,
We endured.
Drank water
From a hole in the ground,
Ate saltless, stolen potatoes,
(While concocting fantasies
about food recipes).

The Abandoned

We dreamed
Of sitting down to a meal,
Of taking off our clothes,
Of warm water and cleanliness.

At night,
Under cover of darkness,
Walls of green,
And towering canopies of trees,
We often chanted prayers
And sang songs,
Ending with our favorite,
Zol Shoyn Kumen Di Ge'uleh —
Let the redemption come soon,
Urging God to see to it,
Lest the Messiah come
 "A little bit too late."

Begging

Meekly, she went into the village.
A dozen houses strung along the road,
Scrawny pigs walloped in the mud.
One poor peasant woman had pity and gave
A homespun cloth, buttonless caftan
Full of tears and patches,
And even the patches were threadbare in places.
From another she got a short piece of rope,
Wound it round her waist as tight as she could,
So it wouldn't come apart
Should she suddenly have to hide.
Both kind women said,
"Better you should have died
With your parents,
Than be a child alone
In these merciless times."

Now in her newly acquired coat,
Lice invaded each fold.
She scratched herself wildly
Until she bled.
And from all the filth and neglect
An infection plagued her shorn head,
A crusty scab of festering sores.
She kept it under a remnant of cloth,
A piece of a Russian parachute
Dropped for the underground.
"My kerchief," she said proudly,
"A partisan's gift."

Her feet bound in rags
Inside sandals of bark,
Pulled on tightly, ready to run.

"Are there still places on earth,"
She'd contemplate,
"Where children play in open spaces
And are not afraid?"

Stepanetchko

A man in his forties,
A poor, illiterate peasant
With a kind face,
A merciful disposition,
And deep knowledge of lore,
Becomes our teacher,
Our rescuer.

Pine tar extracted from trees
Cures our wildly itching rashes
All over,
Between fingers and toes.
Urine on a leaf
Cleanses our torn arms and legs.
A straw moistened with saliva
Coaxes the flea from inside the ear
Where, trapped, it leaps
And drives us crazy.
He digs a hole in the ground for water,
Teaches us to comb the forest
For edible mushrooms and berries,
Roots, grasses and vines,
Distinguish sounds,
Identify foliage,
And tap maple trees
For their sweet sap.
He even teaches us how to beg.

In a home spun, embroidered
Russian peasant shirt,
Worn over patched trousers,

A tattered sheepskin coat
With a rope for a sash,
Feet encased in *lapti*,
Sandals made of bast,
Atop rag footbindings,
Laced with a rope
That twined about the calf,
Over his pants, and up to his knees,
Stepanetchko came
Into densest forest growth
With his willing ox
Harnessed to a wooden cart,
To help us build a hideout.

Stepanetchko lived
In a humble cabin,
Straw filled the crevices
Between bare logs,
With uneven dirt floor,
Under a thatch roof.
In the corner of the back wall
Stood the huge, clay oven,
And a wooden plank bed,
Covered with straw,
Ran along the rest of it.
In the other two corners
Were an old hand loom,
And a crudely carved,
Wooden table ➡

With benches all around.
Opposite the plank bed
There were two small windows,
Like eyes,
Looking unto a clearing
With its vast wilderness beyond,
A ready refuge
In time of danger.
A Russian icon hung
Between the windows,
And hand embroidered linens
Adorned the holy image.

Sometimes we'd have a meal
With Stepanetchko and his family.
A pot of boiled potatoes
Was emptied onto the table.
We peeled and ate them.
When the cabbage borscht
In the communal wooden bowl
Was almost consumed,
He would collect the adults' wooden spoons,
Shake them over the bowl,
Lest a drop be lost,
And give the rest
To my sister and me
Because we were little, he said,
And couldn't keep up
With the grown-ups.

In the evening
The burning kindling
Hissed and sputtered

And lit the room,
Filling it with the smell of pine.
We sat around it
Spinning, knitting,
Working the shuttle of the loom,
And carving wood,
As we sang
Their native songs.
Our voices co-mingled,
And I felt close to them.

'Twas my turn
To stay over
To help
With seasonal chores.
After nightly prayers,
The family,
And their helpers,
Slept together
On the planking
Covered with straw.
We lay so close,
When one turned
Everyone had to move,
The straw was noisily redistributed,
And underneath,
The planks bent and creaked.
The cabin air was barely breathable...
Yet, even a castle
Would not have been
More special
To me. ➡

Stepanetchko lived only
On what he was able to produce
With his capacity for work
And his physical strength.
He would talk to his ox
Of his sorrows.
We promised to help ease his lot
After the war, if we survive.
But the Germans, attempting
To cut off support
To partisans hiding in the woods,
Razed whole villages and farms
On the outer fringes of the forest,
Killing thousands of peasants.
Stepanetchko and his family,
His ox, his cow, his dogs
Were shot to death,
And his farmstead
Torched.

Swallowing a sob,
We picked through the wreckage,
And found Stepanetchko's
Blackened,
Fire damaged
Ax and saw,
He so recently used
To build our hideout.

Winter, 1942

After escaping death in the ghetto
The forest concealed us unconditionally,
Offering refuge, and its bounty
With unlimited kindness,
Though captive, we were also free...

Then, winter gripped the forest,
Life was put on hold.
We huddled amid evergreens,
Naked trees with sparkling limbs,
Layers upon layers of purest snow,
Driving wind, and numbing cold.
At dusk the vast primordial forest
Lapsed into solemn stillness,
Broken only by distant howling wolves.

But the unappeasable, murderous Germans
Came on skis to "cleanse" the woods.
We abandoned our tiny hut with glowing embers
For the deeper wilderness,
And felt safer
After freshly falling snow
Obliterated our tracks.

Ears were poised to identify every sound,
From falling trees to snapping twigs.
And day by day we kept from starving
With scraps of food we had begged, and saved,
And prayed they should outlast the Nazi sweep.

Trees

From the shadows in the forest
We suddenly see the light of a clearing
Through the trees up ahead,
And suddenly we're in it.

Stately trees stand aligned in a circle,
Rising in huge columns
To majestic heights.
The shaggy crown of every tree
Thrusts upward still,
Closer to God,
As if to petition,
And pray for us,
Swaying back and forth
Like grown-ups
In the synagogue.
Sunlight, unfiltered,
Floods the clearing
With a golden hue,
And for a moment,
A sense of communion
Vies with abandonment.

Embraced as trees of life,
At odds with human atrocities,
They bend backwards
To protect and sustain us,
Like our God of yesteryear.

O you compassionate trees,
Our only chance to live
Is with you
In your labyrinth.

The Abandoned

Stealing Potatoes

During two years of hiding in the woods,
Foraging, begging, and stealing,
Hunger is ongoing.
Mushroom and berry harvests are short lived.
Begging helps little,
The peasants themselves are destitute.
The best means to fight starvation
Is stealing potatoes.

In the dark of night,
Crawling on all four,
We edge up to the boundary of a field,
Burrow our hands under a potato plant,
And dig...

Vicious watchdogs fiercely howling,
Indifferent to our hunger,
Rouse the farmers.
They come flying from their dwelling,
Night shirts flaring,
Shaking fists, yelling and swearing.

Swift as high winds
We outrun the howling hounds,
Tightly clutching the stolen spuds.

Hunger Won Out

To Russian Orthodox believers
Eggs represented the resurrection
At Easter.
Hard to come by, precious,
They boiled them, and saved them,
And left them as offerings
On family grave sites.

We searched the cemetery
That very night.
Father's booty was
The hard boiled egg
My sister and I shared.

The peasants felt sure
The disappearance of their offerings
Was a miracle from God.
We kept our truth.

Hunger won out.

Back in Lachva, 1944

She lay cradled on a sack of straw,
On a narrow, wooden cot,
Warped planks and loosened nails.
It wobbled and creaked
Every time father propped her up
To coax her to sip some of the soup
He managed to make
From vegetables and bones
He had begged,
Desperate to fight dehydration
And her raging dysentery.

What hellish irony,
After all she had endured
To succumb now
And die
Of this insidious disease.

And in her desolate, gloomy town,
Funeral bells clanged every day,
Victims of the epidemic.

Father nursed her ceaselessly,
Silently,
Whole nights at her side.
At long last, frail,
And weak,
He had her on her feet.

In the tarnished mirror
She saw her hairless scalp,
A creature faint and worn,
Much too old looking to be a child.
She felt a staggering sense
Of being at once,
Dead and alive.

Final Solution

There are no Jews in Lachva any more,
Or in Lenin, Luninetz and Kozhangorodok.
No chanting in wooden synagogues,
No Sabbath candle lights in windows,
No "Next year in Jerusalem" hopes.

There are no cobblers or tailors hard at work,
No water carrier, midwife or matchmaker,
No Rabbi, poet or "homespun" philosopher.

In each *shtetl* without its Jews
There hovers roaring silence
Testifying to the truth.

Displaced Persons:
Camp Föhrenwald, 1945

The Polish landscape with its villages
Vanishes into the past
Even as we look.

We hoist our bundles onto
The deck of a flat car
Of an endless, moving freight,
Hurl ourselves onto that platform,
Hanging on for dear life,
As the train picks up speed.

Houses drift by
With lighted windows,
Smoke rises from chimneys.
We can't imagine the lives
Of the people inside.
Only our existence seems real.

It is important to leave Poland
With all possible haste,
Before the Communists establish control
And close every route of escape.

Carrying the Poland of our childhood
Inside of us,
We arrive in the American zone,
In west Germany,
Where we exchange our status
Of Polish citizens
For that of Displaced Persons.

Memories of My Father

World War II was not a war,
It was m u r d e r.
The Germans decreed
Jews had no right to life.
We died at their hands.
Only my father, my little sister and I,
Kept our lives.

Dad was resurrected
To be our savior
During two years of hiding
In the woods,
And we survived
Through his unbounded love
And sacrifice.

Though powerless to quiet
Our empty bellies with food,
Or shelter us from cold,
He was a symbol of life and healing
Amid nothing but hatefulness and death.
(And he found his strength in us.)
The healing power of his hand
Stilled our every pain –
Toothache, earache,
Or unbearable fear.

And, he had concern
For children left alone.
Some even owe their lives to him...

Father went sleepless night after night
Watching over us and tending the fire,
Lest a spark ignite
Our tinderbox of a shelter.

On May 24, 1946
He brought us to America,
To provide us
With a human future, he said.
Fighting hunger and death
Staked a claim
On daddy's health.
And soon, the ravages
Of Parkinson's Disease
Ended his every striving.
How we sorrowed at his state...

Frail and weak,
In his love for us
He was still a titan.

With no notion of entitlement,
He urged us to live quietly
And modestly,
And be content.
Not to laugh too loudly,
Or want too much.
If you're alive, he said,
What more can you ask? ➡

Be grateful
That you live
In the United States.

In 1966, at 68,
Daddy passed away.
A broken man,
A *saint*
Gone straight to heaven.

Those at his nursing home bed
Misunderstood his slurred, last words.
It wasn't "the chicken" he tried to say,
We know for certain,
He said "the children."

I flung a spadeful of gravel
Onto his grave.

Learning "American"

You came from a Displaced Persons Camp
To a new land, at last
A place of permanence.

Eager to acquire the language
And American idiom,
You turn to radio, and television.
The traffic update comes on:
"There's been an accident in the Bronx,
And now the traffic is bumper to bumper
Due to rubbernecking on the soft shoulder."

Most expressions you get somehow,
But this one, you just can't figure out.

The Power of Fear

She met death face to face
In fresh pressed SS garb.
It impaled itself
In her mind,
And still
Breaks into her thoughts
At will.
She sweats and trembles,
Her heart shakes,
She loses contact with people,
Faces are blank,
She ceases to be rational,
And hungers for air.

Where she lives,
In the Bronx,
She hears a sniffing dog,
Unmuzzled, (of course),
And (booted) footsteps
Ascending the stairs.
Terror races below her skin.
She hides
And waits
For the danger to pass.

The Abandoned

The World Stood Silent

How could it be possible
That the earth continued to spin,
That somewhere there were weddings,
And births,
Baptisms and Bar Mitzvahs,
Feasts to celebrate,
And photographs
To savor happy memories,
Even as the Nazis
Decreed our fate?

And how could it be possible
That so much inhumanity and barbarism
Be concentrated in one group of people
And their collaborators,
Who beat and tortured to death
With personal brutality and sadism?

That the world stood silent,
That suffering and death
Continued uninterrupted?

That already there are those
Evading and denying facts
My own eyes witnessed.

How could it be possible?

Haunted

Lost
She begs police for help,
They roar, full throated laughter,
That a Jew-kid should even dare.

Then, a command in German,
"HALT!"
Searchlights glare in the dark,
Hands grip her throat,
Her heart tears itself
Into pieces
Against her ribs.
Dying,
She wills herself to gasp for breath.

Blood stains the earth.
Machine guns rattle.
She moans and sobs in sleep.

In Place of Them

In dreams I see
My childhood friends,
White floating clouds
Become heavenly angels.

As I reach out to touch
Each familiar little face,
To pour out the words,
"I'll keep your memory
All of my days,"
They sway, and sway,
And vanish in mid-air.
How long I linger
And stare.

We ran for our lives
Under German fire,
They fell,
And I go on.
I wake tormented,
I live in place of them.

Reparations

Now they give us money.
How many German marks
For a mother,
A sister,
And twenty five other family members
M u r d e r e d?
Wiedergutmachung they call it —
Setting things right.
Their reparations can no more solace us
Than they can bring our loved ones
Back into life.

No matter how long we live,
Our lives are diminished.
Even joy is sorrowful.

Shoah Legacy

I don't believe that man is trustworthy,
Or that God is just and merciful.
I don't believe that the murdered
Have no voice.
I don't believe that surviving is living,
Or that nightmares aren't real,
Or that Shoah grief can be consoled.
I don't believe that we Jews
Brought our fate on ourselves,
Or that anti-Semitism is of the past,
Despite some signs of tolerance.

If this ancient hatred is indeed
S u b s i d i n g,
Why are incidents rising
Everywhere?

Visitations

Memories come pouring forth
At night,
As if only darkness befits that
Horrid source,
Which has irrevocably dimmed my life.
Waiting for sleep in my bed,
Nightclothes drenched in cold sweat,
They
Come gliding through the wall
And hover overhead,
Ghosts
Of my murdered family.
R e l e n t l e s s
Voices In the quiet of the room
Compel me to pay heed to them.

Summoned thus,
My fragile psyche's undermined,
Even as I long for dawn
And light.

Postscript

Every time I remember death,
And I think of it every day,
Would that I could ease the hold
The terrifying past has on me.

At the time I could not grieve,
And now grief won't rescind.
Mourning has become a way of life,
Will it go on without end?

In my daily devotion I pray
For healing to begin in earnest.
I draw a line between now and then
And vow not to cross over.

But sad remembrances and fear conspire,
And try as I may,
I cannot quiet
My mind.

In One Moment I Was Robbed

In one moment I was robbed
Of family, home, friend and faith,
Became locked in the grip of that moment
For the rest of my days.

I believe in remembering,
As if it is even possible to forget.
But to confront the Shoah fully
Is akin to madness.

"Look to time," people say,
"To blunt your frightful memories!"
But the distance of more than fifty years
Has not diminished their poignancy.

And will a hundred years, or more,
Unburden my remembrances?
Or will they retain their power
And reach beyond the grave?

The Abandoned

Summing Up

Nazi tyranny
Annihilated family.
Resisters' bravery
Produced my destiny.
New philosophy,
Anti-Godly.
Sad eternally,
Soul in humility,
Waiting for epiphany.

Confronting God: A Monologue

The world was a raging hell.
Facing annihilation,
We implored You to intervene.
You kept silent.

Your people, the orthodox elders,
Who lived most righteously
And kept Your every commandment,
In their unwavering faith
Opposed violent resistance.
They went to their deaths
Unvalued, unnoticed,
Believing it was You
Who summoned them.

Our young people,
Against hopeless odds,
Staged a bloody uprising,
Created my chance to flee.
But if I was kept alive
By Your design,
Does the miracle of my survival
Compensate for the many killed?

Where were You when gold teeth
Were ripped from jaws,
When women and children were shot
And buried half alive?
You kept silent.

I've been afraid to speak harshly to You,
And even now I hesitate
To pour out my rage.
It should not surprise You, though,
That I, the witness,
Cannot reconcile Your existence
With the slaughter of innocents.
Can one go through hell
And continue to trust
In Your goodness?

And yet, I *want*
To come to terms with You,
Experience You as present.

But for the record,
There will always be
In the convex mirror
Of the Shoah,
The likeness of me,
Eyes bursting toward Heaven,
Mouth pried open
By a scream.

Past Present

A light, a sound,
A word, a smell,
Trigger vivid images
From that distant
Horrifying past.

Suddenly I am a child again
In the grip of fear and death.
Unable to unload
The memories of hell,
To shed the
Hair shirt that I wear,
Half-a-century after the fact
The mind is still obsessed with them.
And this mind-set
Stays stubbornly fixed.

Past Perfect

Again and again
I'm in that open field behind our house.
My mother's footsteps next to mine.
She leads off with her beautiful voice,
And we sing softly
As we pick wild flowers
And twine them into garlands.

I see those blossoms now,
And deeply inhale that
Fragrant, pure air,
And I know what love is,
And calm, and delight.

I must have been seven,
Or maybe eight,
For when I was nine
War came
Abruptly changing normalcy
Into dark foreboding.

Sabbath Afternoons

The further into the past they recede,
Those golden Sabbath afternoons
With close knit family,
The dearer they become.

Grandparents, uncles and aunts
Occupy the many chairs
Around the ready laid festive table,
Set with glasses in silver holders,
Coal-fired, meticulously polished,
Brass samovar,
With tea leaves steeping atop,
And plates of fruit, cookies and cake
Mother herself had made.

Grandpa Sholom with his vest pocket watch
Dangling from the chain
Crossing over at the waist,
Its face with Roman numerals,
Challenging us to tell time.
Grandpa Yankl spinning his magic tricks,
Making things disappear and reappear.
The grandmothers and aunts,
Looking their lovely best,
Telling about the great-grandmothers
For whom we are named,
How charitable they had been,
And how they lived by God's commands.

Familiar voices talking softly,
Loudly, laughter.
My two sisters and I
Reciting poems, singing songs,
And winning loud applause.

In silence, where I keep my losses,
I hear their laughter and their words.

Childhood Memory

One somber Autumn night
After my older sister had left home
To study at the *gymnasium*,
I lay in the room we had shared
Staring at her empty bed,
Minding the storm outside.

The weeping willow, impelled by the wind,
Lifted its branches and flung them
Against our tin roof, back and forth,
With sounds reverberating inside.
Rain thrashed against the windows,
And the flickering light
From the kerosene night lamp
Filled the room with moving shadows.
Suddenly the light went out.
Frightened of the dark, I cried.
Father rushed to me,
Held me in his arms,
Relit the night lamp
And lay down beside me
Till restlessness subsided
And passed into sleep.

How could I have known then
That the recollection of that scene
Would hold in it such cherished memories,
That the world the tin roof sheltered
Would soon be lost forever.

The *Abandoned*

Credo

Nothing is casual since then.
Things to be taken for granted
– My very senses –
Loom as miracles to me.
Oh, the smell of bread,
The taste of salt upon my tongue,
The sight of children, my very own,
And the sweetness felt at holding them.

I over-react to injustice,
The world cannot be trusted.
Evil hearts, desperately hardened,
Indifferent to human suffering,
Are bent on destruction.
Neither the wicked, nor the virtuous,
Receive due justice.

And yet,
 I am moved to tears in gratitude
By the slightest act of kindness,
A sympathetic gesture,
A compassionate word...

What good is the lure of possessions,
In a flash they can be lost.
I revere humanity, knowledge and skill.
These cannot be confiscated or enslaved.

And all the time I know that death awaits.

Faded Photographs

I long sought and found
Some family photographs from home
Sent to the U.S., Canada and Palestine,
 Inscribed and dated in the twenties and thirties.
One is in mother's elegant handwriting.

Their images are carefully placed
In an album with silken cover,
Each labeled,
Lest they go unnamed
When it's time to pass on
The task of remembering.

The blurred, beloved faces
On my aging photographs
Validate who I was, and
Who I am still.
They give stability
To my life
Interrupted by war and Nazis,
And divided between two worlds.

The last to have known them
To have witnessed "liquidation"
– The brutal murder of my people –
Mother and sister,
Grandparents to infant cousins,
Kinfolk, all of them
Lost to the Germans.

My children, too, are defined by my losses.
We look at the pictures together.
I explain who is who:
"Your grandma, killed at thirty-six,
Your aunt, at sixteen,"
In the hope that they will remember,
And pass on our story
To those who come after.

Talk Therapy

You're much too serious,
You seldom smile,
You anticipate adversity,
You're apprehensive all the time.

Re-examine your philosophy,
Not even God can change the past,
While you have time on your side
Invest it with some cheerfulness.

Happiness is not a thing apart
That is beyond your grasp.
Take heart, and finely integrate
A little gladness
With the sadness of your past.

Dichotomy

"You're so resilient,
Not a trace of your past,
You're teaching English,
Having earned your degrees,
A suburban housewife
With a husband and two kids,
You go driving, shopping,
Meeting all your needs."

But gestures of normality notwithstanding,
My reel of memories is endlessly unwinding.
Voices come to me strangely
Demanding they be heard,
Beckoning and beckoning,
Transcending my veneer.

My two worlds are out of harmony,
My life without serenity.

Untitled

Some say, "Put it behind you!"
What a soulless concept
To put it behind!

Decades after the event
Something in me cries out,
It's the presence of the absence
Of family and friend.

Loss has given my life its shape.
All that I have and haven't become
To that cruelest time I can trace.

Support Group

We know why your poems are sad,
Why you can't write of happiness.
WE understand...

Pray keep your tears in check,
No one must detect
Your sadness.
Feign cheerfulness at any cost,
Or chance the hurts of loneliness.

The world won't seek to soothe your pain,
So go on, do what you must do!
Then bring your heavy heart to us,
And we will share with you
Survivor's lot.

Motherpoem

No one ever cooked for me
Planned my meal deliciously
Pondered over spices
Considering what I liked
Stood over the oven hot
Watched and skimmed the pot
Reduced the flame to simmer
Placed it under cover
Hoped to do it perfectly
Just for me
Just for me

First Day of School

I see a little girl
Lunch box at her side
Neatly groomed
White socks
New shoes
Mother kisses her good-bye
Then waves
The school-bus pulls away

I feel a tug
An image flashes through my mind
I want to hug
That little girl inside
From the ghetto and the forest
But the cars behind
Keep honking me onward

I Want to Be Free

I want to be free,
Rid of nightmares,
Military uniforms,
Black boots,
Motorcycles and airplanes.

I want to close the ghetto
And the forest door.

I want a sense of wellness,
To laugh without restraint,
Be wild and crazy,
And feel good about it.

I want some magic power
To reach inside my head,
Teach me to, at once,
Remember and forget.

Aftermath

Fifty years after the fact
Painful memories intact
Nightmares recurring
Nazis appearing.

Must survivors remain
At their altar of pain
Forever enduring
Unspeakable haunting?

And will it subside
On life's Other Side,
Or go on persisting
Into the realm of night?

Elizabeth Sarah, July 25, 1996

I snuggle her tightly in my arms,
She listens to my lullaby.
I know this child,
She has my eyes,
And the family tendency
To wrinkle her brow.
"Don't analyze, just love her!"

They had a plan for me to die,
My life went on.
My older sister perished,
She was just sixteen,
She continues to be,
This child carries her name.
"Never mind the why and how!"

Deepen your hold
On the here and now,
Shout yourself hoarse,
"I am a grandmother!"

But there is that voice within
That lives my life along with me;
"By what reason or what right
Are you the one
To have retained
The gift of life?"

My joy is joy confined.

The Abandoned

Reunion: Lachva Ghetto Survivors Israel, June 1998

Wish it had been possible
To put my arms around each of you,
Sit together, one on one, for hours,
Hear your story of survival,
How you managed to go on
Alone,
And how the years have been to you,
To share memories of home
And family,
Of loss and pain,
To name names...

Instead we met just fleetingly,
In a restaurant,
Collectively.
Devastated –
How few of us remain,
Marked by the Shoah
And its aftermath.
But overjoyed, too,
With each familiar face.

Then midnight came,
And we, again,
D i s p e r s e d.

Thanksgiving 1998

Seated at a table of plenty,
Surrounded by children
And grandkids,
I conjure up an image,
And the image persists:
Starving children
Hiding in the forest
Foraging for mushrooms
That sprout after rain.

Oblivious to water running
Down our faces
And soaking us to the skin,
We slog through the dripping woods
Searching for mushroom bouquets.
We put them on a fragment of clay pot,
Rescued from a farm
Germans had destroyed,
Placed it by the open fire,
Let them drown in their own juice,
And their succulent texture
Is like heaven on the tongue.

These sturdy fungi lived hidden lives
In ankle-deep moss, rotting leaves,
Around stumps and under trees,
Thriving in their dank environment.

Now they're grown
In plastic containers,
In high-tech lighted labs,
In standardized sizes.

Mushroom fanciers recommend
They be sauteed with ingredients,
Or glazed with balsamic vinegar,
For that "mysterious woodsy flavor."

No matter all the winds of change,
The mushrooms of my childhood,
And I,
Still hide.

Monument at Moriah

There stands a monument
In memory of the innocent.
Children huddled together
Rigid with terror
Peering through windows
They can never enter.

These mute stone forms
This courtyard now adorn,
Their each and every size
To sounds of bells gives rise.
Like the devout processional
Of a holy funeral
The throng winds its way,
Bells suspended in the breeze
Endless *Kaddish* prayers say.

The oven doors were open wide,
The world slept through this horrid rite.
Forsaken, left to their own device,
A million children lost their lives.

These bells toll for the living
To avenge the children's murder:
"As long as you go on remembering
We shall endure."

Written upon seeing the monument at the Moriah School in
Englewood, N. J. in memory of the children who perished. It
consists of slabs of Jerusalem stone in assorted sizes. Each is
partially hollowed and with a bell suspended within. The sculptor
is Edward T. Jacobs.

The *Abandoned*

Fragments of Memory

It begins with a wedding,
Or a funeral procession.
The entire Jewish community
Of the *shtetl*
Is present.
Or, the little boy crying
Throughout the first night
In the ghetto,
Ich vil di nechtige heim!
I *want yesterday's home*!

It could be the longing for bread.
It could be shadows in the forest
Where branches overlap
And sunlight never enters,
Or unending snowfall
And blustering winds.

Then there's father's handwriting
On an old letter,
With that special patina
It has acquired,
Or mother's photograph
Inscribed in 1935.

I'm always back
To my beginnings,
Precluding any possible
Lightness of being.

The Red Dress

I always wanted
To don shocking red,
But ended up wearing
Black and gray instead.

I wanted to have
A sense of belonging,
But felt disconnected
At every crossing.

I never have heard
The music of life
Without remembering
Its darkest side.

But very recently
I half realized my quest,
Though I haven't yet worn it,
I bought a red dress.

My parents, Menia and Moshe-Zev Romanowsky.

My older sister, Esther, (on the right), with cousin Lea Romanowsky.

The Romanowsky family. Seated from left is Rivke Romanowsky Fishman with her two older children, Henie and Yoske. Next to her are her parents, Genieshe and Sholom, their two sons Moshe-Zev and Berl (standing) with his wife, Feigl.

The Rabinovitch family. Seated from the left is Moshe-Zev Romanowsky with his oldest daughter, Esther, Menie, his wife, and her parents Nechama and Yankl with their two sons (standing) Shmuel Ber and Gershon.

Feigl, first row center, and husband, Dov Lopatin, seated behind her to the left, (was head of the *Judenrat*).

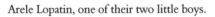

Arele Lopatin, one of their two little boys.

The Rokchin family. Seated on the far left is Yitzhak, (organized and led the ghetto uprising).

Yosele the water carrier with his son.

Here I am (bottom row) with my sister Esther and the entire student body of the Bet Hasefer in Lachva, 1936.

German military belt buckle inscribed with
"God is with us."

Lapti (in Russian). Bast sandals woven from the
bark of reeds. They are soaked in water to make
the bark strips pliable.

Entrance to Föhrenwald, Jewish Displaced Persons Center.

My father, Moshe-Zev, my sister Genia and I (on the right) enroute to Camp Föhrenwald, Germany, 1945.

My father, my sister and I (on the left) upon arrival in the United States, May 24, 1946.

Lachva Revisited

July 9 – July 18, 2001

Lachva Revisited

We meet up with our tour to Lachva and to four small adjacent communities at the Belarus Hotel in Minsk on Tuesday, July 9, 2001. It consists of 41 people, mostly second and third generation from Israel. The older people in the group had fought in the Russian army, with the partisans, or both, and found their families gone when they returned to their homes. Kopel Kolpanitzky, the tour's organizer, who now lives in Israel, is originally from Lachva. He has organized these trips for the last eleven or so years as a labor of love. He and I were the only survivors of the ghetto uprising, and were to provide the rest of the group with first hand details. My cousin, Yoske Fishman, with his photographic memory would also supply many details about different families, location of their homes, who is related to whom, etc.

The next day we travel in our tour bus to Luninietz. It is a larger town not far from the communities we will visit, and has the only hotel in the entire area. We check into the Hotel Yubileinaya, and my husband, Norbert, and I are assigned to Room 319, on the third floor walk-up. It is small, unclean, the bed sheets are patched, the bedspread dirty, and the furnishings unbelievably worn. The bathroom produces only a trickle of cold water. There are separate communal showers for men and women on the first floor, which will have hot water available by the weekend. Later we attend a reception by the District Commissioner and festive dinner. There are speeches in Russian and Hebrew, and I too am asked to say a few words.

It is now Thursday. We have breakfast at a nearby restaurant at which we are joined by some of the politicians who met with us the night before, and group pictures are taken. Next we travel to the monument in Luninietz which has been placed at the mass grave where 4,932 Jews had been killed. Very moving commemoration ceremonies are held with speeches and with prayers. This is repeated at every other site we visit. Mass graves dot the landscape.

Finally we arrive in Lachva. The commemoration ceremonies at the grave site here are extremely emotional especially because the largest number of people on the bus came to visit Lachva. As a surprise for us, the town had placed a series of plaques over the entire length of the grave listing the names of those buried here. The Lachva contingent from Israel brought a list of names of all who had perished here to read out loud.

Lachva is nothing like it was when Jews lived here. From a thriving town in Poland (now Belarus), it has turned into a forsaken, drab, dismal place devoid of vitality. The area where the ghetto once stood has never been rehabilitated after fire set during the uprising destroyed it. It is overgrown with weeds and unrecognizable. The old market place, much reduced in size, is also neglected. In the center is a monument dedicated to the Soviet Unknown Soldier of World War II, or the Great Patriotic War, as it is called here.

Our home no longer exists, and has been replaced by a small, simple little house. I am not sure of the lot it had occupied, but the man across the street knows where it was. He introduces me to the present owner, and I get her permission to look around our back yard. I ask if she had heard of the Romanowskys. "Of course" she replies, " my house stands on their property."

Soon I meet a woman who remembers my older sister, Esther. She describes her perfectly. She remembers my family as "the richest Jews in town," as "good people who even sold to the peasants on credit."

Now I meet Olga Romanovna who had been my friend when we were little. We have a very moving reunion and recall our childhood together. She brings me homemade wine, and bread, and a lovely needlepoint of a forest scene. We exchange addresses and vow to stay in touch.

I have two especially meaningful moments. One was when we stopped at a grave by the roadside where 24 partisans lie buried together under a monument bearing a Soviet Red Star. Among them is one Jew, Dov Lopatin, the dedicated head of the *Judenrat* in Lachva. When all Jewish men in the entire area were killed, he negotiated successfully with the Nazis to let the Lachva men live and continue as slave laborers. And, on the day when the ghetto was to be liquidated, it was he who gave the signal for the uprising to begin by setting fire to the house where the *Judenrat* functioned. Lopatin escaped during the uprising, and joined the partisans. On his final mission he stepped on a land mine and was killed. It was April 1944, just three months before the liberation. How privileged I feel to stand at his place of burial.

The other incredible moment comes when we visit the Jewish cemetery in Lenin. I notice that one of the graves is that of Pisarevitch, who died in 1984. He was a Jewish partisan who helped us a lot during our two years of hiding in the forest.

I ask the mayor about him. The mayor knew Pisarevitch, describes him perfectly and tells me that he had been a true hero who had performed many brave deeds, and had received much public recognition.

The trip is extraordinarily successful primarily due to Kopel's organizational skills, and his intimate knowledge of the area and its people. Great diplomatic skill is required, since everything that is done, including the maintenance of the grave sites and monuments, and every appearance of politicians and entertainers had to be rewarded to the satisfaction of those involved.

I have long rejected the thought of going back to Lachva, afraid to relive my past. But with the advent of time, I needed to be at the Mass Grave at least once in my life. The fact that my cousins, Yoske Fishman and Jacob Bukchin, were going, and that it was Kopel Kolpanitzky, a fellow ghetto survivor, who was leading the group, helped a lot. Though it is a deeply emotional and disturbing experience to return to the place which holds such painful memories for me, I am extremely glad to have revisited Lachva.

The Mass Grave

Off the bus
And into the past.
Out of the secular
And into the sacred.
Something incomprehensible
Had happened here.
Something so enormous,
The mind can't grasp it.

Nearly sixty years after
That day of murder,
September 3, 1942,
I set foot
On this abandoned field,
Walking hesitantly up
The graded, shallow hill,
Afraid to confront the Mass Grave,
Even as I long to be close to it.

2,000 innocents
Are enwombed in this earth:
Mother and sister among them,
All of my grandparents,
Eight aunts and uncles,
Nine cousins,
And everyone dear.
(Here, too, death had expected me.)
I'm theirs, and they're mine.
We are inextricably entwined.
So many flashes,
Imaginary hugs and kisses, ➡

And tenderness,
And anger, and rage,
And images of bloody carnage,
All mixed in.

Here I am
Standing motionless with the others,
(Though my memories divide us),
Heads bowed,
Observing a moment's silence,
Lighting memorial candles
Against the sudden wind that rises,
Reciting the *Kaddish*.
A sea of chiseled stone
Spans the grave.
Fifteen black tablets
Across its entire length
Identify those buried here.
Prostrate,
We finger the letters
Of our loved ones' names.

I want to believe,
I must believe,
They died running
During the ghetto uprising.
Or, were they driven
Over the little wooden bridge
Across the river,
Past the Greek Orthodox Church,

Cupolas and squires intact,
Over the last stretch
Of dirt road
To face their executioners?

No plant or shrub
Relieves this spot.
"None would grow
In soil soaked with blood,"
The caretaker said.
"I tried."
Just some withered,
Dried up flowers,
Someone put here long ago,
Ride the gentle breeze.

Would to God
That I could have my way,
Take every one of them
Out of here,
Enshrine them
Where a beaten footpath
Would replace
This trackless field,
Even as Moses,
Upon leaving Egypt,
"Took the bones of Joseph with him..." *

*Ex. 13:19.

Lachva Revisited

Lachva Now

Nothing looks familiar.
Where are the landmarks I knew,
Our house,
The water well,
The weeping willow?

I struggle
To find my bearings,
When some insane energy
Propels me to run
Down our empty street,
Screaming inwardly:
"Don't you remember,
I was a little girl here
With my family?"

The passers-by are few.
I stop a peasant woman,
One old enough to know:
"*Babushka*," I plead,
"Where did you used to buy fabric?"
"Why, at Romanowsky's textile store.
Wonderful people they were,
Even sold us on credit.
The richest Jews in our village.
Your father, so handsome,
Like a Polish *pan*.
I remember, I remember all of them."
Tensed, I listen.
I could have kissed her.
Our existence here is affirmed.

The *Abandoned*

I feel heady...
"How did you save yourself?" she asked.
"The ghetto uprising, I ran."

She says she was my older sister's friend.
"We're both from 1926.
Her name was Esther.
She wore glasses.
—Prettier than you,
Tiny nose, light hair."
I listen intently,
Careful not to prompt her.

Another woman, Olga, continues:
"You sat next to me in school
Under the Soviets, remember?
We danced together, sang songs,
Recited poems in praise of Stalin.
You were a star then, in 1939."
She brings me homemade bread, and wine.
We hug and talk all day,
And her recollections
Validate my memories.

Official receptions,
Balladeers, vodka and feasts,
Collide with an impulse to tears.

Sixty years worth of weeds
Rise over the ashes
Of the ghetto streets,
And in the depth of this serene landscape
There lies a solitary Mass Grave.

The Old Cemetery

Not a tombstone remains,
Only rows of mounds,
Unidentifiable,
Some barely visible,
Just the rise and fall of the land
Beneath my soles.
My great-grandparents
Are somewhere here.
Their spirit hovers
Amid the weeds.

In my subconscious vision
They're in their Heavenly abode,
Capable of knowledge
Of this world.
They know
That I'm here,
In this empty expanse,
Searching for a sign of them,
That peasants plundered the monuments
For paving their yards,
That pressure from survivors
Thwarted plans
To cultivate this land,
That this Old Jewish Cemetery
And the site of the Mass Grave
Each acquired status of National Monument,
And a fence,
And that unaware, stray cattle
No longer trod or graze
Our holiest of places.

How I wish
I could identify
My ancestral graves,
Touch the Hebrew letters of their names,
Learn exactly when they lived and died,
Find evidence that once,
In a long-ago time,
We really were here.

My paternal great-grandparents, Chaja-Sheindl
and Leibke Romanowsky. Both died in the late
1930s.

Partisan Pisarevitch

We hide in the forest
At the side of the partisans.
One of them discovers us.
He brings all he can
Because there are children,
Be it cow's intestines
That partisans discard
Or a remnant of cloth
From a Russian parachute.

In a well worn Soviet uniform,
A rifle slung over his shoulder,
Mustache curled upward
(ala hero Chapayev),
He is optimistic about survival,
Makes us smile
Gives us hope.
He sings with us old songs,
And teaches us new ones
About life and death of partisans.

We lost one another
After liberation, in 1944.
Now it's 2001,
I am on a pilgrimage to Belarus,
Where I was born.
While roaming the old cemetery in Lenin,
I come upon a tombstone bearing his name:
PISAREVITCH, SAMUIL EVSEEVITCH
1908 ~ 1984.
I rush to confirm that he is the one,
Sasha, that wonderful partisan

For whom we always waited
During two years in the forest.
With my arms around his monument,
I recount, out loud, his kindnesses.

I M A G I N E!
After fifty-seven years
I "meet" Pisarevitch.
Finding one another
Is not just for the living.

1942 - 2002

It's sixty years since then,
And I still don't understand:
Who gave evil man
Dominion over fellow-man?
Was it the world
Unconcerned with our fate,
Or Heaven too high
For our pleas to be heard?
Not a sea was parted,
Nor was there manna dispensed
In the wilderness.

Abandoned,
Our boys revolted,
Brought down the ghetto's
Barbed wire fence,
But T H E Y themselves
Never got out.
For some unknown reason,
I survived.

I see the world
And everything in it
Through the prism
Of that experience,
Taste the silence
That hovers there,
Shun the living daylight,
And beg for dreamless nights.

For some unknown reason, I survived.

The Abandoned

With Kopel Kolpanitzky, fellow ghetto survivor and tour leader, 2001.

With my two cousins from Israel, Yoske Fishman and Jacob Bukchin (right).

Commemorative plaque at the Mass Grave. The Hebrew and Belorussian
inscription reads as follows in translation:

SACRED GROUND

HERE ARE BURIED THE JEWS OF LACHVA

AND SURROUNDINGS

1650 - 1942

At The Mass Grave. Photograph by Gershon Volochiansky.

With my husband, Norbert, at the roadside burial place of 24 partisans. The last name listed here is that of Dov Lopatin, (head of the Lachva *Judenrat*), the only Jew. The Russian inscription on the plaque reads as follows in translation:

HERE ARE BURIED PARTISANS OF THE KIROV BRIGADE, OF THE PINSK DISTRICT. ETERNAL GLORY BE TO THESE HEROES WHO DIED FIGHTING FOR FREEDOM AND INDEPENDENCE OF OUR HOMELAND.

Reunion with Olga Romanovna, (on the left).

The only thatch roof house remaining in Lachva as of July 2003.
Photograph by Gershon Volochiansky.

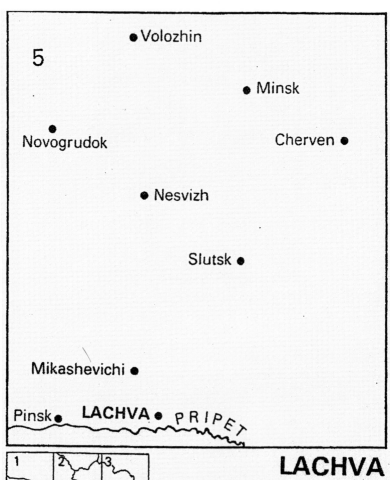

5

Volozhin

Minsk

Novogrudok

Cherven

Nesvizh

Slutsk

Mikashevichi

Pinsk   LACHVA   PRIPET

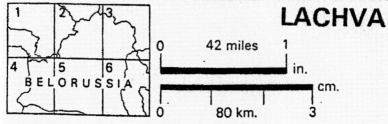

LACHVA

| 1 | 2 | 3 |
| 4 | 5 | 6 |

BELORUSSIA

0   42 miles   1
                         in.
                         cm.
0   80 km.   3

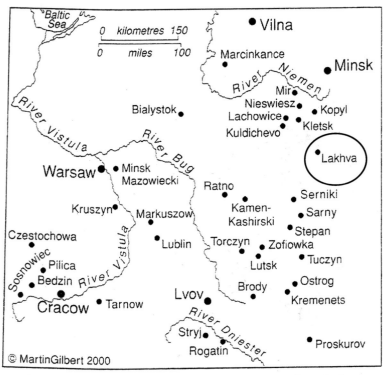

Map showing some of the ghettos in which Jewish revolts took place.